PRAYERS
FOR THE SEASONS
OF GOD'S PEOPLE

PRAYERS
FOR THE SEASONS
OF GOD'S PEOPLE

Worship Aids for the Revised Common Lectionary, Year C

B. David Hostetter

ABINGDON PRESS
Nashville

PRAYERS FOR THE SEASONS OF GOD'S PEOPLE:
WORSHIP AIDS FOR THE REVISED COMMON LECTIONARY, YEAR C

Copyright © 1997 by Abingdon Press

All rights reserved.

Cataloging-in-Publication data applied for with the Library of Congress and available upon request from the publisher

97 98 99 00 01 02 03 04 05 06— 10 9 8 7 6 5 4 3 2 1

MANUFACTURED IN THE UNITED STATES OF AMERICA

Contents

After Pentecost

Preface

When I served as a pastor in the Presbyterian Church in Canada, I frequently used James Ferguson's *Prayers for Common Worship* (London: Allen & Co., 1956). Particularly as a pastor faced with the task of leading morning and evening services for a number of years, I often turned with appreciation to Ferguson's book, which began with the following inscription:

Morning and Evening
Every Lord's Day
Throughout the Course
Of the Christian Year

With the use of newer translations of the Bible, I found it necessary to update the language of my public as well as my private prayers. Thus began the composition of a collection of prayers geared to the Revised Common Lectionary which I have used in my own ministry. Using Ferguson's book as a guide, I have now completed this annual cycle of prayers of invocation, confession, thanksgiving, dedication, intercession, commemoration, and prayers of the day, and have included one-sentence introductions to the lessons for the day. Having used them weekly for some time myself, they are offered here in the hope that other pastors and leaders in Christian worship will find them of benefit.

B. David Hostetter

Advent/Christmas

First Sunday in Advent

First Lesson - The prophet promises justice and righteousness in the days to come that will bring salvation and safety to God's people. Jeremiah 33:14-16

Psalm 25:1-10

Second Lesson - The apostle Paul hopes specifically for the return of Christ with his saints. 1 Thessalonians 3:9-13

Gospel - Jesus is not only a teacher, but on occasion an apocalyptic prophet, making dire predictions. Luke 21:25-36

CALL TO WORSHIP

Leader: The grace of our Lord Jesus Christ be with you all.

People: And also with you.

Leader: Be vigilant, praying at all times for strength to pass safely through all imminent troubles.

People: We will be vigilant and ready to stand in the presence of the Son of Man.

INVOCATION

Eternal God, be present to our prayers by the Spirit so that we may lay aside our anxieties and cares in your worship, and prepare our souls for your judgment and mercy in Jesus Christ our Lord. Amen

PRAYER OF CONFESSION

God of all history, the passing of time sometimes escapes us. We live from payday to payday, from party to party, from crisis to crisis. We lose sight of our spiritual state of health until illness or tragedy brings us up short to take stock of ourselves again. We escape as we can from the social ills of our time, without seeing that they are signs of the times. Forgive our frequent indifference to the state of the nations and the immaturity of our souls, for the sake of your perfect Son, Jesus of Nazareth. Amen

Declaration of Pardon

Pastor: Friends, hear the Good News! God is confirming your heartfelt belief

People: so that we will stand faultless with all those who appear with Jesus before our Maker.

Pastor: Friends, believe the Good News!

People: In Jesus Christ, we are forgiven.

[AND]

Exhortation

Keep awake and sober. The Son of Man is coming with great power and glory. Hold your heads high, for your liberation is near.

PRAYER OF THE DAY

Eternal One, who was, who is, and who is to come, keep us aware of the meaning of events in our own lives and in our times. Save us from panic that hinders our doing anything constructive in society and thwarts personal growth. Save us from the fear that no service we offer will be good enough. Be our ruler day by day. Amen

PRAYER OF THANKSGIVING

God of the prophets, righteous sovereign, Child of David's line, we rejoice in the branch of David that springs up and that buds and blossoms again and again with justice among the nations. We are excited by every victory of truth over falsehood, every triumph of compassion over indifference, every return of those who have gone astray. We live in hope of the final perfection of your world in your time. Amen

10

PRAYER OF DEDICATION

God our Savior, we stand before you as those who are ready to be led by you in your way, to use what we have to clear the way for the coming of your goodness in full measure, through Mary's son, Jesus, and in the Spirit of the Christ. Amen

PRAYER OF INTERCESSION AND COMMEMORATION

Heavenly Parent, your Son Jesus taught us that we need to pray always and not to lose heart. Hear, then, our intercessions in the name of our Lord Jesus.

First we pray for your own household, which is the church, the pillar and bastion of the truth. Strengthen it with the power and unity of the Spirit that its sincerity and love may not be gainsaid. Sustain all the leaders of your church in the world. Stir up your church here and in every land and make us worthy of all that Christ has done for us. Purge the church of all that is contrary to the truth of Christ and subversive of faith, love, and unity. Having pruned away all deadwood, make us truly fruitful branches of the Vine which is Christ.

Encourage all Christians to give up any dishonorable dealings, and to work honestly, so as to have something to share with the needy. In their daily work may no evil talk come out of their mouths, but only what is useful for building up, as there is need, so that their words may give grace to those who hear and the Holy Spirit not be grieved.

Help all husbands and wives to honor the bonds of wedlock and guard the sanctity of the home, the basic link of human society and the honored symbol of the union of Christ and the church. Give parents joy in their children and support in their heavy responsibility as guardians and teachers of the young. Teach all children to honor their parents and every member of the family to serve one another in love.

Bless those who make our laws, those who execute them, and all who govern us nationally and locally. May they be worthy of our honor by ruling justly and without fear or favor. Save society from corruption and civil strife. Bring a spirit of cooperation among us that we may all seek to serve the common good.

We pray for all who are weary, worn, and sad, for those are in agony of body, mind, or spirit. May they heed our Savior's invitation to come to him for rest. Give health to the sick and strength to the weak. To those who are near to death give the faith of Simeon, who seeing your salvation in Jesus Christ was ready to depart in peace according to your Word.

Everlasting God, we remember before you with gratitude, our beloved and sainted dead, who having served you in earth now worship and serve you around your heavenly throne. Grant us grace to labor as they labored in faith and patience of hope, that hereafter we may also come to higher service with all your saints, through Jesus Christ our Lord, to whom with you, O God, and the Holy Spirit be given unending thanksgiving. Amen

Second Sunday in Advent

First Lesson - The message of this messenger is that the Coming One will purify the temple as a refiner purifies precious metal. Malachi 3:1-4

Luke 1:68-79

Second Lesson - The sharing of the gospel is a great joy to both the preacher and the congregation. Philippians 1:3-11

Gospel - John the Baptist preaches a baptism of repentance as a way of preparing the way for the coming of the Christ. Luke 3:1-6

CALL TO WORSHIP

Leader: The grace of our Lord Jesus Christ be with you all.

People: And also with you.

Leader: Get the road ready for the royal visit: make a straight path for Christ to travel!

People: The winding roads must be made straight and the rough places smooth. All humanity shall see God's salvation.

INVOCATION

God our Savior, we turn our wandering minds to you and seek a new vision of your love and direct guidance from Jesus Christ by the Spirit. Prepare us to celebrate the first coming of our Lord Jesus and to do your work in expectation of his Second Coming in power and great glory. Amen

PRAYER OF CONFESSION

Holy God, Messenger of the new covenant, flaming Spirit, we confess that we are sinners and cannot worship you worthily except as we are purified and cleansed of our sins. Let your Holy Fire refine our characters, and not merely our appearance, so that our very natures can become true and rich, purged of the dross of our deepest faults and the evil that corrupts us. Fit both pastor and people to worship you in the purity appropriate to the house of God, through the fire of the Holy Spirit. Amen

Declaration of Pardon

Pastor: Friends, hear the Good News! The One who started the good work in you

People: will bring it to completion by the Day of Christ Jesus.

Pastor: Friends, believe the Good News!

People: In Jesus Christ, we are forgiven.

13

[AND]

Exhortation

Grow richer in love, in knowledge and insight of every kind, then on the Day of Christ, you will be flawless and without blame, reaping the full harvest of goodness that comes through Jesus Christ to the glory of God.

PRAYER OF THE DAY

In this year of our Lord, in this day of our times, Speaker-Out-of-Eternity, let your word be heard again, that every baptism may be a sign of repentance for the forgiveness of sins, and the wilderness of modern life bloom with the flowers of goodness and peace. Amen

PRAYER OF THANKSGIVING

Turner-of-tides, you have done great things for us and we are glad indeed. Out of illness we have found new health. Out of sorrow we have found new rivers of joy. In barren places we have planted seeds that you bring to a harvest of goodness. Out of spiritual poverty you have restored our fortune and made us rich in Christ. All praise to you! We sing for you! Amen

PRAYER OF DEDICATION

Receive, Divine Harvester, our offerings as seed-money that enables the sowing of the seed of the Word in this place and to the ends of the earth. Use us as your hired hands, busy both in sowing and in harvesting, for the sake of Christ's church. Amen

PRAYER OF INTERCESSION
AND COMMEMORATION

Faithful God, as you promised the blessed Virgin Mary a Son to be given the throne of his ancestor David to reign over

14

the house of Jacob forever, and of whose kingdom there will be no end, so fulfill the promise of salvation to your people with the final victory of his kingdom in the earth. Hasten the day when all nations shall serve you and we need pray no longer, "Your kingdom come."

God of Israel and the church, your temple in Jerusalem was called a "house of prayer for all peoples," but needed cleansing by the Messiah when he found people "making it a den of robbers." Make the church everywhere a pure temple for your Spirit and a worthy house of prayer for the nations. Everywhere cleanse your church from all defilement, reforming whatever is false and unworthy of you. Enliven your people where lethargy has set in and where lukewarmness in worship and service disgraces your cause.

We pray for our country, its leaders and elected officials at every level of government. Bless our land with educators who have a love for truth.

Inspire our artists, writers, composers, musicians, and all who participate in the lively arts that a vision of beauty may again capture the public imagination. Give to captains of industry and commerce an understanding of the public good beyond the profit-making goal.

We pray for our homes, our kith and kin, near and far from us. As every household has its needs and every person some weakness, hear the prayers of all your people. Be friend and guardian to our children. Give strength to those who are sorely tempted. Grant health to the sick, comfort to the bereaved, rest to the aged, and peace to the dying.

Eternal God, who received your Son Jesus again into glory and by your messengers promised that he will come in the same way as he was received into heaven, hasten the coming of that day when sin and death will be vanquished and we with all your faithful departed will be perfected in blessedness to the glory of your rule.

And to you, our God, who is and who was and who is to come, the Almighty, be ascribed glory and dominion forever and ever. Amen

Third Sunday in Advent

First Lesson - The coming king is forecast as strong against oppressors but a savior of the disadvantaged and the outcast. Zephaniah 3:14-20

Isaiah 12:2-6

Second Lesson - Paul urges rejoicing since the best is yet to be. Philippians 4:4-7

Gospel - John the Baptist is like a broom sweeping clean the way of the Lord's coming. Luke 3:7-18

CALL TO WORSHIP

Leader: The grace of our Lord Jesus Christ be with you all.

People: And also with you.

Leader: Express gratitude to God, invoking God by name.

People: We will make God's deeds known in the world around, declaring the supremacy of the divine name.

INVOCATION

As your people, covenant God, we are filled with expectation as we approach again the celebration of the first advent of your Son, Jesus of Nazareth, whose coming was heralded by John the Baptist. Inspire us by the hearing of the Good News that we may be spiritually prepared for another encounter with the living Christ, in whose name we pray. Amen

PRAYER OF CONFESSION

God of peace, Prince of peace, Spirit of peace, your names are to be hallowed as supreme. Forgive us if we fail to give due honor to your name in our families and in our social life. In our society the name of Santa Claus sometimes obscures the

16

name of the Christ Child, the hammering of elves drowns out the song of angels. The mission of reindeer competes with the adoration of shepherds and the travel of those who seek the one born to be king. Pardon us if we have let such things get out of hand in our social circles. Help us to restore your name to its rightful place. Amen

Declaration of Pardon

Pastor: Friends, hear the Good News! The peace of God, which is beyond our utmost understanding,

People: will keep guard over our hearts and our thoughts, in Christ Jesus.

Pastor: Friends, believe the Good News!

People: In Jesus Christ, we are forgiven.

[AND]

Exhortation

Now my friends, all that is true, all that is noble, all that is just and pure, all that is lovable and gracious, whatever is excellent and admirable—fill all your thoughts with these things.

PRAYER OF THE DAY

God of wisdom, God-in-action, Spirit of inquiry, prompt us to ask not only what we should believe but what we should do. Save us from fruitless speculation that does not issue in obedient action to fulfill our vocation to serve you in the serving of others. Amen

PRAYER OF THANKSGIVING

Magnanimous God, to the cries for help we have made in anxious moments, and the petitions we have offered in times of need, we add our thanksgivings and our expressions of joy. We have joy in the Lord because you have enabled us to put into practice some of the lessons that Jesus and the apostles have taught us, and to follow the good example of others, old and young, who have also been following Christ. We have no higher joy than the sense of your presence and the love you show us again and again. Amen

PRAYER OF DEDICATION

Holy One of Israel, Christ of the church, we gather here as sons and daughters of the faithful, to make our deeds known in the community where we live, and to declare that your name is supreme. We depart to take our cup of joy to share with others, in the name of Jesus. Amen

PRAYER OF INTERCESSION AND COMMEMORATION

Founder of the church, to this end we pray to you, that you will make your church worthy of its calling and fulfill by your power every good resolve and work of faith to the glory of your name. Continue to send your messengers to the remotest people on our globe that your way may be known upon earth, your saving power among all nations.

We pray especially for your church with new opportunities of growth in lands where doors and hearts have formerly closed to the Good News are now open. Grant that the church may never deaden the conscience of your people but in the Spirit of the Christ make them alive and loving to all. Arm with the sword of the Spirit and the shield of faith all who challenge strongholds of wickedness in the name of Christ. May they overcome resistance with kindness and, steadfast in the faith, speak the truth with love against all reproach. So may the rule of Christ be extended as the disobedient comply with your commandments, repenting of their rebellion against you and your law.

We pray for our country and all in authority over us. Direct and enlighten their consultations for the public welfare that all may be ordered in accordance with your just law and our common life be more equitable and harmonious, that there may be respect for all informed opinion and religion, free elections and wise dialogue in civil matters.

Gracious God, having sent your Son to lift up the lowly and fill the hungry with good things, send your church in helpfulness to accomplish the same mission in our time and place. Send your people to sympathize with the suffering, care for the sick, feed the hungry, cool the fevered brow, and comfort the anxious and bereaved. May our faith in Christ be evident in our compassion for others.

We rejoice, eternal God, in your gracious provision for all your saints departing this life with their hopes in your incarnate Son, who in death and resurrection promised that we should live also. Following those who were our companions and guides in the way of Christ, may we have a peaceful death and enter with joy into the heavenly place our Lord Jesus has prepared for his followers. May your name be hallowed, heavenly Father, divine/human Brother, motherly Spirit, one God, for ever and ever. Amen

Fourth Sunday in Advent

First Lesson - Bethlehem is the unlikely birthplace of one who, though newly born, has existed from ancient days. Micah 5:2-5a

Luke 1:47-55
[OR]
Psalm 80:1-7

Second Lesson - The coming of the Christ is the offering of the supreme sacrifice to replace any other less adequate offerings for human sin. Hebrews 10:5-10

Gospel - The meeting of Elizabeth and Mary, both mothers by special arrangement of the Creator, is an occasion of great joy and thanksgiving. Luke 1:39-45 (46-55)

CALL TO WORSHIP

Leader: The grace of our Lord Jesus Christ be with you all.

People: And also with you.

Leader: After the example of Jesus Christ in his coming, present yourselves before God.

People: We say: "I have come to do your will, O God."

INVOCATION

We bow before your throne, Sovereign of sovereigns, with the intention of hearing your Word and doing your will. Grant us the aid of your Holy Spirit, that we may fulfill our intentions; through Jesus Christ our Lord. Amen

PRAYER OF CONFESSION

God of surprises, you bring your name of peace out of a small clan and a previously insignificant place. Wrongly we have looked for you only among the powerful. If we have stood in the way of those you have called to be shepherds of your flock because they did not seem imposing and appeared in humility, we are sorry. We need to measure greatness as you do, as manifest in Jesus Christ, in whose name we pray. Amen

Declaration of Pardon

Pastor: Friends, hear the Good News! God has not resisted the prayers of the people.

People: God's face shines on us in Jesus Christ, that we may be saved.

Pastor: Friends, believe the Good News!

People: In Jesus Christ, we are forgiven.

[AND]

Exhortation

Recount what you have been told about this child Jesus, and share the real meaning of what has happened in Bethlehem.

20

PRAYER OF THE DAY

Give us joy in believing, God our Savior, that as you have kept past promises, you will also fulfill those for the future made by your Son, Jesus Christ. Give us joy in believing that our children and grandchildren may live to see that great day if it does not come in ours. Amen

PRAYER OF THANKSGIVING

Responsive God, you have restored your people who have called upon you. We have prayed that you would make your face shine upon us, that we might be saved. Your response has been to become human for humanity's salvation. We rejoice with the apostle, that we have seen the light of the knowledge of the glory of God in the face of Jesus Christ. With Elizabeth we share the wonder, "Who are we, that the mother of our Lord should be one of us?" With blessed Mary, we rejoice in God our Savior. Amen

PRAYER OF DEDICATION

Receive your church standing before you, O God, as a body prepared to be moved by the Spirit to do your will in our time and in this place. Amen

PRAYER OF INTERCESSION AND COMMEMORATION

God of eternity, Lord of time, timeless Spirit, hear our prayers for the whole human family.

Incarnate God, from adorable infancy in Bethlehem's manger you have shared our human adulthood and mortality to be exalted again to the glory of heaven to hold in your right hand seven stars as the angels of the churches. From your mouth have come sharp words of judgment and loving words of forgiveness. Fortify the faith of the church by the witness that you are the first and the last, the living one, who

21

was dead, but is alive again forever and has the keys of Death and of Hades. Save your people from the sentimental Christmas that misses the meaning and glory of the gospel. As we approach again the celebration of your first advent, may we give clear witness as to who stands knocking on our doors this season.

May our love for the baby in the manger be multiplied by your Spirit to include all children, especially the children of the poor, children who are sick, babies born into addiction and abuse. Send appropriate help to parents struggling to care for their little ones. Bless every social agency dedicated to serving human need in any form.

Open the hearts of unbelievers to the Good News even when the Christmas story is told glibly in media often casual if not irreverent. May the doubtful, the rejected, the unloved, find your good will from members of your church as well as the choirs of heaven.

At this season of childlike innocence bring a cleansing wave of repentance across the life of our nation washing away impiety and the corruption that is rampant and the deceit that is hidden. Let truth and justice with mercy be the stability of our nation. Preserve our freedom to hear the Good News of Jesus Christ amidst the clamor of many voices and many ideologies and religions.

At this season of celebration bless and comfort all who are alone, those without any family, those who are at a distance from their families in reality or by dispute. Reconcile the disaffected, raise up the sick, console those who mourn, deliver the tempted and tried through the help, comfort, and salvation of Jesus Christ.

Heavenly Parent, we rejoice that you have given as a gift to your Son all whom you have loved from endless age, all those chosen in Christ before the foundation of the world to be holy and blameless before you in love. By your unmerited grace, receive us also in our time to be with them in your glorious kingdom through Jesus Christ to whom with you and the Holy Spirit be all glory and praise. Amen

Christmas Eve/Day
(First Proper A, B, C)

First Lesson - In the darkness the prophet welcomes the light of the great king in the line of David who will bring justice and peace. Isaiah 9:2-7

Psalm 96

Second Lesson - The grace of God that was made personal in Jesus Christ is expected again. Titus 2:11-14

Gospel - In Bethlehem, a shepherd's town, is born the Savior who is Mary's little Jesus, a descendant of the great king, David. Luke 2:1-14 (15-20)

CALL TO WORSHIP

Leader: The grace of our Lord Jesus Christ be with you all.
People: And also with you.
Leader: Silence, everyone, in the presence of God.
People: God has come out of the sanctuary of heaven in Jesus Christ.

INVOCATION

God of mystery, God of revelation, God of joyful sound, we worship you with the most profound devotion, and with the simplest wonder at the foot of a manger bed, singing in the Spirit so that our joy may be received as true worship; in the name of Jesus Christ. Amen

PRAYER OF CONFESSION

God of all worlds, ours seems at times like an abandoned one. We share in its sin, its darkness, and its despair. We feel that you have left us alone to find our own way out of the mess we have made of things. We have forgotten that the world was created by you, re-visited by you in Jesus Christ, and is still yours, a dwelling place of your choice for your Spirit. Forgive the belief that you are nowhere, that forgets that you are now here, in the Spirit of Jesus Christ. Amen

Declaration of Pardon

Pastor: Friends, hear the Good News! The Lord has come, and is coming again.

People: Let the peace of God keep guard over our hearts and our thoughts, in Christ Jesus.

Pastor: Friends, believe the Good News!

People: In Jesus Christ, we are forgiven.

[AND]

Exhortation

The Lord is near. Have no anxiety, but in everything make your requests known to God in prayer and petition with thanksgiving.

PRAYER OF THE DAY

Child of Bethlehem, Man of Nazareth, Christ of God, with Mary we treasure the stories of your birth and ponder over these things. May the celebration of your birth, both in this place and in our social circles, bring glory and praise to your name. Amen

PRAYER OF THANKSGIVING

Shepherd of Israel, Lamb of God, Keeper of Christ's flock, with Bethlehem shepherds of old, we come to see what has happened and consider what has been made known to us. We rejoice in the birth of this child Jesus who embodies both the good Shepherd and the Lamb of God that takes away the sin of the world. For his obedience to your saving purpose we are thankful. That you become involved in the sin and suffering of our world, we are astonished. That you continue

24

to draw us together as your flock by the Spirit we are comforted. Amen

PRAYER OF DEDICATION

Not often enough, O God, do we offer you the gift of our silence, in adoration, in attentiveness, in anticipation of your directions. Receive us in this solemn moment, and in such times of silence as we find for you in the days to come. Amen

PRAYER OF INTERCESSION
AND COMMEMORATION

Gracious God, you have set your holy child in our midst and taught us through him that unless we turn again and become as little children we cannot enter into his kingdom. Give your church always the spirit of lowliness and love that we may never offend any child of yours however weak, but honoring every human being, as Jesus did, may we share the inheritance of his light and truth with all who will receive it.

Bless our land and every land that all nations may live in the freedom to honor your name by faith and obedience. Bless the United Nations that it may be an instrument of your peace, serving to reconcile nations in conflict, and inspiring human rights and the care of little children everywhere.

Deliver those members of the church who are under persecution where religious freedom is limited to another religion. Save us from the use of political power to coerce religious faith. Give us faith in the power of your truth to persuade the unbelieving and the doubtful. Grant us the blessedness of being peacemakers.

Head of the heavenly family, from whom every family in heaven and on earth takes its name, we pray that every family will be a truly holy one. Hallow our homes by the prayers of our families and our love for each other. As Jesus took children into his arms to bless them, may we see that no child is left parentless or without proper care.

We pray for the poor, the sick, the sad, for all who are homeless, lonely, or abandoned. Send us to them to relieve their loneliness, to ease their suffering, and to cheer them. Grant your healing and help for those beyond our capacity to help. Sustain in unclouded faith the dying, granting them eternal rest and ultimate joy.

Everlasting God, we rejoice that with you are the spirits of the righteous made perfect, the assembly of the firstborn who are enrolled in heaven. By your grace in Jesus Christ receive us when we come to this life's end, into the rest you have prepared for your faithful people. Bring us at the last to what we now hope for in Christ our Savior. To God our Savior be given all thanksgiving and endless worship. Amen

First Sunday after Christmas Day

First Lesson - Samuel, the young assistant to the priest, Eli, grows physically, spiritually, and socially. 1 Samuel 2:18-20, 26

Psalm 148

Second Lesson - Paul describes the attributes of spiritual maturity to which we should aspire as committed Christians. Colossians 3:12-17

Gospel - Like Hannah's Samuel, Mary's Jesus reaches the age of inquiry and decision-making. Luke 2:41-52

CALL TO WORSHIP

Leader: The grace of our Lord Jesus Christ be with you all.

People: And also with you.

Leader: Give thanks to our Sovereign with your whole heart.

People: We will give hearty thanks in the company of the entire congregation.

INVOCATION

Sovereign God, it is fitting that we seek your presence in the company of our neighbors as well as in our private prayers for you are our Creator and Savior. Receive the worship we offer through Jesus Christ our Lord. Amen

PRAYER OF CONFESSION

Ageless God, forgive us if we have kept the young from worshiping with us by our insistence on old ways of worship and our refusal to accept new forms of worship and praise that can involve children and youth with us in our gathering. Excuse our demands for stillness and silence that ignore your acceptance of children in their simplicity and sincerity. By the examples of Samuel and Jesus, open our minds to the service that can be rendered to you by the young in years and the young in heart. Amen

Declaration of Pardon

Pastor: Friends, hear the Good News! God has forgiven you.

People: We will let the peace of Christ abide in our hearts.

Pastor: Friends, believe the Good News!

People: In Jesus Christ, we are forgiven.

[AND]

Exhortation

As you have been forgiven, be forgiving, compassionate, kind, humble, gentle, patient, preserving the unity of the church as the body of Christ.

PRAYER OF THE DAY

Child of God and child with human parents, teach us to grow in wisdom, both by listening and by asking questions. Help us to keep in proper balance our duties to the church family and our own households that we too may increase in favor with God and our peers. Amen

PRAYER OF THANKSGIVING

Mind beyond our knowing, we praise you for revealing what we should know in Jesus Christ. Treasure beyond our possessing, we give thanks that for the sake of our enrichment, Christ shared human poverty to put divine wealth within our reach. Maker of history, who can trace your purposes? We marvel at your ways with humanity, and live in suspense as to the future you point to in Jesus Christ, Child of history, Child of eternity. Amen

PRAYER OF DEDICATION

We are not so foolish, wise God, as to believe that we can buy your favor with these gifts. We make our offering and present ourselves a living sacrifice, that your will be done on earth as in heaven. Amen

PRAYER OF INTERCESSION
AND COMMEMORATION

Ancient of Days, Unaging Christ, Ageless Spirit, as you have been with us in the year that is past, go before us in the year about to begin.

Maintain your church in faithful witness to the truth in your Son, Jesus Christ, and zealous in its ministry to all humanity. Give us grace and power in the sight of all peoples, and bring into deeper unity all who love one Lord and baptize in your name, Father, Son, and Holy Spirit.

Strengthen your church everywhere in the world that the ignorant may be enlightened, the idolatrous and superstitious freed from their fears, and those in need ministered to in the name of Christ. Gather to your church all your wandering children to the glory of your name.

Bless with health, wisdom, and courage, our national leaders. Guide and empower all councils and authorities in just action for the good of all. Cleanse and reform our politics and laws, our education, commerce, and art, that justice may prosper and people share fairly in the good things you have created and in the enjoyment of what is good and beautiful.

May it please you, O God, to console the bereaved, to grant patience and hope to the suffering and health to the sick. Provide for those in need through both public and private and church agencies so that in serving them Christ will be honored and served.

Eternal God, we give thanks for your grace and virtue manifest in all your saints, especially for those who in this year have ended their time with us and have been received into glory. As we remember them, may we commit ourselves again to follow their good examples, living steadfastly in your church and in continuing communion with all your faithful people and prophets, apostles and martyrs in every year of our Lord. To you, fatherly, brotherly, motherly God, we ascribe all honor and glory now and forever. Amen

Second Sunday after Christmas Day

First Lesson - The eternal Shepherd gathers his diverse and hurting flock. Jeremiah 31:7-14
[OR]
Wisdom has a place of honor in the divine purpose. Sirach 24:1-12

Psalm 147:12-20
[OR]
Wisdom of Solomon 10:15-21

Second Lesson - Paul gives praise to God for the timeless plan that includes the Ephesians and himself. Ephesians 1:3-14

Gospel - The Good News is that God came to us in Christ so that we might come with Christ to God. John 1:(1-9), 10-18

29

CALL TO WORSHIP

Leader: The grace of our Lord Jesus Christ be with you all.

People: And also with you.

Leader: God turns mourning into gladness,

People: God gives joy to outdo our sorrow.

INVOCATION

God of our hopes, Christ of our faith, Spirit in our hearts, we come to worship you with joy and gladness. Your goodness knows no limits; you are kind to all and we worship you in all sincerity; through Jesus Christ our Lord. Amen

PRAYER OF CONFESSION

All-glorious God, paternal, fraternal, maternal, though we have faith in Jesus Christ, and love toward your people, yet we are not without blemish in your sight. Our love is not as inclusive as yours, and there is much we need to learn. Give us a clearer vision of all that we are meant to be, so that by becoming fulfilled, we may increase the glory that is properly revealed in Jesus Christ, your beloved. Amen

Declaration of Pardon

Pastor: Friends, hear the Good News! The liberator has come to free us from all proud pretenses.

People: The Christ has come in Jesus of Nazareth to show us the undeserved favor of God.

Pastor: Friends, believe the Good News!

People: In Jesus Christ, we are forgiven.

[AND]

Exhortation

Accept the limitations of your own knowledge. Have reverence for the wisdom of the Creator. Be thankful for his love in Christ and for a humble place in his house.

PRAYER OF THE DAY

Available God, whatever our age, whether married or single, make us sensitive to what you are doing and about to do, that we may not miss the excitement of being a part of the living history that you are writing, through Jesus Christ. Amen

PRAYER OF THANKSGIVING

We give thanks, God of Job and Jeremiah, David's Lord, Anna's Christ, Luke's Savior, that we have found your house in many places. We have found places of prayer with the swallows and the sparrows. We have sung your praise in a quiet circle under the stars. We have enjoyed the choir of many voices and the joyous sounds of musical instruments and found inspiration and refreshment. Along our pilgrim way you provide the cup that sustains both soul and body. We are happy when we trust in you. Amen

PRAYER OF DEDICATION

God of all places, many of us return to this place again and again, expecting spiritual refreshment and growth in grace. Bless all that we do to make this a place of renewal for all who will come to Jesus Christ. Amen

PRAYER OF INTERCESSION
AND COMMEMORATION

Mighty God, hear our humble prayers on behalf of the world you love and for which you sent your special Son, Jesus Christ.

Remember your one holy universal church. Sanctify and build up your people that being saved from error and super-stition and worldliness, they may ever hold the mystery of faith in a pure conscience.

Remember this congregation of your church. Grant us new visions of truth, new zeal for your honor, new members

31

to increase the numbers of people to serve you and our community.

Deepen our joy in the love of Christ, in secret and in public prayer, in our love of neighbor. Anoint us by the Spirit that we may be refreshed in our service for another year. By prayer and by gifts of money make us partners in prayer and witness with all missions and all agencies who serve you in the name of Jesus Christ.

Remember all whom we have elected to govern us. Strengthen them in their commitment to truth and justice that prejudice and favoritism may be put aside. Give us to see more fully liberty and justice for all.

Remember all upon whose daily labor we depend and especially those seeking gainful employment. Grant us economic leadership that is as concerned with the need for employment as for the profits of corporations and their stockholders.

Remember all who negotiate between conflicting nations or parties that we may enjoy a new measure of peace in the earth.

Remember all who stand in special need of your help, stricken by illness or accident, especially those dear to us whom we name in our hearts. Be rest to the weary, health to the sick, comfort to the bereaved, friend of the lonely, the light of the wandering, the hope of the dying, the Savior of the lost.

Eternal God, we recall with thanksgiving that we are surrounded by a great cloud of witnesses, the great company of the redeemed in heaven, especially those who departed this life in the past year. Let us also lay aside every weight and the sin that clings so closely, and let us run with perseverance the race that is set before us, looking to Jesus the pioneer and perfecter of our faith, who for the sake of the joy that was set before him endured the cross, disregarding its shame, and has taken his seat at the right hand of your throne, O God, to whom with you and the Holy Spirit, we give all humble worship. Amen

*E*piphany

First Sunday after the Epiphany (Baptism of Our Lord)

First Lesson - The prophet reassures the people of God of the commitment of their Creator to their survival and growth. Isaiah 43:1-7

Psalm 29

Second Lesson - In the season when we remember that Jesus Christ is revealed to the Gentiles we are reminded that the Spirit also will be given them in the course of events. Acts 8:14-17

Gospel - Though he is a cousin of Jesus, John the Baptist gives full recognition to Jesus as one whose role is infinitely greater than his own. Luke 3:15-17, 21-22

CALL TO WORSHIP

Leader: The grace of our Lord Jesus Christ be with you all.

People: And also with you.

Leader: Praise God's glorious name.

People: We will bow down before the Holy One when Christ appears.

INVOCATION

Strip away inattention and fuzzy-mindedness, O God, that our worship may be attentive and thoughtful and your word heard in clarity and decisiveness; through Jesus Christ our Lord. Amen

PRAYER OF CONFESSION

Magnificent Creator, we are humbled by the voice of your power and majesty. Even your Son Jesus awes us, as he does your servant, John the Baptist, so that we know we are unworthy to unfasten his shoes. We are often too proud to stoop to the menial service that our neighbor's needs require. Forgive the arrogance that overlooks the Christ when he is in the guise of our needy neighbors anywhere in the world; through Jesus Christ, your model Son. Amen

Declaration of Pardon

Pastor: Friends, hear the Good News! We share the promise of God with his people the Jews, through the secret of Christ.

People: Though we are unworthy, we are granted God's favor also in Jesus Christ, and are baptized into the church of his beloved Son.

Pastor: Friends, believe the Good News!

People: In Jesus Christ, we are forgiven.

[AND]

Exhortation

Do not lose heart. Proclaim the Good News of the riches of Christ to all, so that the wisdom of God in all its varied forms may be known by everyone.

PRAYER OF THE DAY

Creator divine, you have planted the seed of the Word within us, so that we may be wheat for your granary. Drench us with the good rain of your Spirit so that we may be part of your abundant harvest to be gathered into your heavenly granary, and not chaff to be destroyed as worthless; through the grace of your worthy Son, Jesus of Nazareth. Amen

PRAYER OF THANKSGIVING

Gracious God, you send your Anointed to bring good news to the poor, to heal the broken-hearted, to announce release to the captives and freedom to those in prison. Such salvation turns sadness into joy and mourning into gladness. So we sing your praise and give thanks to you from sincere hearts, for even in the midst of earth's ruins you help us to rebuild with hope. Amen

PRAYER OF DEDICATION

You are our Monarch forever, O God. We worship you in the presentation of our offerings. Mighty God, give strength to your people, that they may serve you always. Gracious God, bless your people with peace, that they may be peacemakers in a world of strife; through Jesus, Prince of Peace. Amen

PRAYER OF INTERCESSION AND COMMEMORATION

Mighty and eternal God, the brightness of faithful souls, you brought the Gentiles to your light and made known to them the Christ who is the world's true light and the bright and morning star. Fill the whole world with your glory and show yourself in the radiance of light and love to all nations, through Jesus Christ our Lord.

We pray for the good of your church that all who preach may proclaim the truth with love and wisdom showing forth Christ in word and in deed that all may be drawn to him lifted up on the cross.

Stabilize new converts in the faith that their steadfastness may be an example to others who may be on the verge of commitment to you and your church.

Bless our land that there may be peace within our gates and prosperity within our borders. Give grace to our elected leaders that our common allegiance to justice may be strong and the nation confident in the united and mutual support of the people for our common values and vision.

Bless our families and our children. Protect them from cruelty and violence at home, at school, and in their neighborhoods. Renew our commitment to bring up our children in the nurture and admonition of the Lord Jesus.

36

Give health, comfort, and strength to those who are sick, bereaved, or weakened by disease or accident.

Great God, as you led your people through the wilderness to the promised land, so you have led many of our loved ones through the troubles of life into the rest prepared for the people of God. So guide our steps that we may not wander from the way before us in Christ, who is the Way, the Truth, and the Life. To him with you and the Holy Spirit, be all thanksgiving, glory, and praise. Amen

Second Sunday after the Epiphany

First Lesson - The prophet promises the vindication of Jerusalem which has seemed forsaken by God. Isaiah 62:1-5

Psalm 36:5-10

Second Lesson - Paul describes the variety of gifts that the Holy Spirit brings to serve the whole church. 1 Corinthians 12:1-11

Gospel - Jesus brings joy to a wedding feast in Cana when the wine runs out. John 2:1-11

CALL TO WORSHIP

Leader: The grace of our Lord Jesus Christ be with you all.

People: And also with you.

Leader: Come, Christians, worship the One who delights in you.

People: We are not forsaken and desolate. We are called by the new name of Jesus Christ.

INVOCATION

Loving God, we should worship you with the joy of the newlywed for your love is unfailing and unfading, stronger than death, larger than life. We are worthy to worship you only through Jesus Christ in whose church we are his bride. By your Holy Spirit may we always be your holy church to the glory of your name. Amen

PRAYER OF CONFESSION

Faithful God, you have not forsaken us. We have not always been faithful to you. We value your call to virtuous living, but often live at a lower level. We appreciate the fidelity of our friends and spouses, but sometimes betray and abandon them. You give us a variety of gifts to serve you in the church, but much remains undone because we squander the abilities you have given us on less worthy causes. Forgive our erratic service that reflects incomplete obedience, for the sake of your ever-obedient Son, Jesus Christ. Amen

Declaration of Pardon

Pastor: Friends, hear the Good News! Your God rejoices over you

People: as a bridegroom rejoices over the bride.

Pastor: Friends, believe the Good News!

People: In Jesus Christ, we are forgiven.

[AND]

Exhortation

You all have a variety of gifts, but the same Spirit. There are varieties of service. Let us serve the same God.

PRAYER OF THE DAY

Divine Winemaker, the wine you give us at your table is more precious than the wine you made at Cana. We are pledged to do whatever you tell us to do, so that with the whole church we may extend your table to the remotest places in human society, and many may come at the last to the wedding feast of the Lamb. Amen

PRAYER OF THANKSGIVING

Loving God, you give yourself to all of us, to the young and the innocent, to the jaded and the disenchanted, to the tired and the despairing. Your love is like the love of the young bridegroom, like the love of the lonely widower finding a lonely widow, like the love of a king who marries an unlikely commoner. None can be deserving of your love, but all of us can be grateful and return your love with thankful devotion, like your Son, Jesus Christ. Amen

PRAYER OF DEDICATION

Supreme Worker, the offerings we bring have been earned in a variety of jobs. It is our intention that all our work should serve your purposes for all your people. Use these gifts to serve many people in many ways; through Jesus Christ our Lord. Amen

PRAYER OF INTERCESSION AND COMMEMORATION

Hear, O God, our humble intercessions on behalf of all humanity in the name of Christ our Lord.

Send forth your Spirit of truth upon your church throughout the world that all who confess your name may agree in the truth of your Word in writing and especially in the Word made flesh. May we live purely, honestly, and in godly love that Christ may be glorified.

Accompany the messengers of the gospel to every land, and uphold them that they may uplift Christ and hasten the promised time when all people shall know you, their God and Savior.

God of all nations, bless our nation that true religion and virtue may season our common life, that there may be peace within our borders and prosperity for all. Preserve us from corruption, the abuse of power, and unbridled greed. In plenty or in want may we seek first your kingdom and its justice.

God eternal, before whom generations rise and pass away, preserve our sons and daughters in the faith and work of your Son and keep alive the zeal of consecrated youth in the midst of a generation growing old.

Hear us, O God, for all the afflicted and especially for any of our acquaintances who are sick. Sustain their spirits in faith and hope, and in due time make them completely well.

Give comfort to those overburdened with the cares of this life. By the loving and Holy Spirit clear the minds of those plagued by doubt or hatred. Send your people to befriend the friendless and console the bereaved. Give rest and peace to the dying.

Grant that all your children may learn obedience by the things that they suffer, like him who shared our common lot, and having been made perfect, became the Author of eternal salvation to all who trust and obey him.

Almighty God, we praise you that the souls of the righteous are with you and there shall no evil touch them. We bless you for those who have sailed life's seas with us but who have already entered the harbor to which we will come by your grace. Bring us through all storms and contrary winds to the safe and fair haven you have prepared for us through Jesus Christ, both pilot and harbor master, to whom be glory with you, sovereign God, and the Holy Spirit. Amen

Third Sunday after the Epiphany

First Lesson - After exile the recovery of the scriptures during the rebuilding of Jerusalem is occasion for great thanksgiving. Nehemiah 8:1-3, 5-6, 8-10

Psalm 19

Second Lesson - Even the seemingly insignificant parts of the body of Christ are indispensable. 1 Corinthians 12:12-31a

Gospel - Jesus makes his bravest announcement in his own hometown. Luke 4:14-21

CALL TO WORSHIP

Leader: The grace of our Lord Jesus Christ be with you all.

People: And also with you.

Leader: Strive after the better gifts. Christ will show you a still more excellent way.

People: We are the body of Christ, member for member, and will follow the more excellent way.

INVOCATION

Creator of planets and stars, we come to worship you and to seek the guidance we need to keep our lives in the more excellent way. Guide us in our worship and in our daily life, through Jesus Christ our Lord. Amen

PRAYER OF CONFESSION

Living Designer, you have created the church to be one body with many members working together under the control of the Head, Jesus Christ. Forgive us if we have acted toward anyone as if they did not matter, or as if the church could get along without them. Excuse discrimination that gives more praise to some than they deserve at the expense of others who serve modestly without recognition. We do not always share joy and sorrow equally, as we are meant to do. Pardon us for the sake of Jesus Christ who forgets no one. Amen

Declaration of Pardon

Pastor: Friends, hear the Good News! One Holy Spirit was poured out for all of us to drink.

People: The weakest of us is still indispensable to the body of Christ, the church.
Pastor: Friends, believe the Good News!
People: In Jesus Christ, we are forgiven.

[AND]

Exhortation

The Spirit of the Lord has been given to you to preach the Good News to the poor, to proclaim liberty to captives and recovery of sight to the blind. Set free the oppressed. Proclaim this year of the Lord's favor.

PRAYER OF THE DAY

Come alive to us again, living Word, in the hearing of the written Word. Gather us to yourself as we gather to the reading and preaching of the Word so that understanding your will for us, we may go to do it, individually and together. Amen

PRAYER OF THANKSGIVING

God-out-of-hiding, speaking and acting, we rejoice in every rediscovery of your written Word by the hand of prophets and apostles. We are moved to tears when your voice sounds again in our ears after the silence of years. We come to the table   to feast on the rich food and sweet drink that are provided in the sacrament. We give thanks for the spiritual refreshment and inner strength you give us. Let our joy overflow in invitation to others to join us in our feasting; through Jesus Christ our Lord. Amen

PRAYER OF DEDICATION

Spirit of the church, enable us to do what needs to be done, whether little or much, that all of us, doing our part, may help to complete your work in the world. Amen

PRAYER OF INTERCESSION
AND COMMEMORATION

O God, save your people and bless your heritage. Strengthen your servants to continue steadfastly in the teaching of your apostles, in communion with all believers, in the breaking of the bread and the prayers of your church. So may we live and labor in one Spirit and make straight the way of our Lord Jesus Christ.

Light of the world, shine through all your people wherever they may be and whatever their calling, but especially through those who have been commissioned by your church to take the Good News to unenlightened segments of human society. Unite us in our various callings that no work place or social gathering shall be without your spokesperson.

We pray for all who are vested with authority in this and every land, together with their representatives in the United Nations, that there may be justice and peace in our world.

Sustain all who are employed in honest work, and bless those in a position to find work for those who are unemployed that all may know the dignity of work that serves the common good, as did the work of the Carpenter of Nazareth.

Bless our homes with mutual love and peace, with reverence and learning. Bless those who nurse the sick at home or in hospitals and those who take food to the hungry and help to those needing aid.

Bless and guide doctors and nurses, pharmacists, and therapists, that their knowledge of medicine and skill in healing may bring new health and strength to all who need hope and help.

Everlasting God, from whose love nothing can sever us, we bless your name for all your servants who have endured the toils and temptations of this life and are now at rest and in peace with you. Bind us with cords of faith and love to you and all your saints that we may be drawn at last to heaven through the ascended Jesus Christ, to whom with you and the Holy Spirit be all glory, time without end. Amen

Fourth Sunday after the Epiphany

First Lesson - The uncertain modesty of the prophet is overcome with a sense of divine calling to a particular if difficult mission. Jeremiah 1:4-10

Psalm 71:1-6

Second Lesson - Here is the classic definition of Christian love. 1 Corinthians 13:1-13

Gospel - Jesus does not hesitate to tell the truth at the expense of causing controversy that is life-threatening. Luke 4:21-30

CALL TO WORSHIP

Leader: The grace of our Lord Jesus Christ be with you all.

People: And also with you.

Leader: Young and old, give praise to God, who sustains us from childhood to adulthood.

People: We give praise to God, who sustains us through birth and through death.

INVOCATION

Infinite God, we cannot grasp that you are from everlasting to everlasting, so we are grateful that you have come to us in Jesus Christ to make your nature clear to us in a way that can be trusted by the childlike of every generation. Increase our knowledge of you by the teaching Spirit of Jesus Christ. Amen

PRAYER OF CONFESSION

God of all places, forgive us if we are open only to the word of the strange prophet and closed to the truth when it comes from a familiar person. Excuse the pride that discounts what our neighbors and friends can do, assuming that only the distant expert could be wiser than ourselves. Pardon the doubt that prevents doing in our place what others have accomplished in other places but in similar circumstances. We are sorry if we have blocked the advance of the church of your beloved Son, Jesus of Nazareth. Amen

Declaration of Pardon

Pastor: Friends, hear the Good News! God's love lasts forever.

People: There is no place it cannot reach. There is no age it cannot touch.

Pastor: Friends, believe the Good News!

People: In Jesus Christ, we are forgiven.

[AND]

Exhortation

Make love your quest. Prophets' work will end. The ecstasy of tongues will fade. Some knowledge will lose its usefulness, but there will always be the need for love.

PRAYER OF THE DAY

Divine Speaker, let us hear your gracious words from any lips. Divine Healer, let us feel your healing touch by any hand. Let no spirit of doubt prevent your work through our talents or those of others, in the name of Jesus Christ. Amen

PRAYER OF THANKSGIVING

God of love, we are grateful for the love you have shown us in Christ and through other persons, for patience with our failings, for kindness in our weak moments, for praise when we have done our best, for forgiveness without counting the times, for those who go with us when the going gets rough, for those who trust us again after we have abused their trust. For all gifts of love, we thank you, and especially that your love for us is stronger than death. Amen

PRAYER OF DEDICATION

Loving God, we respond to you with such love as we have. Without our heart's love our most generous offering, and even martyrdom, would not make us any better. We want to be even more loving, like Jesus Christ. Amen

PRAYER OF INTERCESSION AND COMMEMORATION

Sovereign God, we pray for your holy, catholic, and apostolic church in all of its branches. As it continues to extend to the corners of the earth, may it mount up in faith, press forward in hope, and rise to the full heights of holy love. Let all who are members of the church show in their lives the gifts of your Holy Spirit, that the nations may come to your light and the kingdom and the power and the glory be yours.

Bless, O God, all who have part in public service. Make them pure in motive, strong in counsel, bold in action, fearing the face of none but doing right in the reverence of your name.

Have mercy, O Lord, upon all who are suffering, the sick and fevered, those in pain and anguish, and those who watch over them with hope and prayer. Comfort the bereaved by their faith in Jesus Christ raised from the dead and ascended into heaven.

Hear the prayers of prisoners who are confined because of their misdeeds. Grant them true repentance and forgiveness and the will to do your will.

Creator and Re-Creator, mend the broken, heal the sick, cleanse the defiled, free those enslaved by addiction. Save us all from our sins, committed or intended.

Eternal God, we remember before you with thanksgiving our fathers and mothers, our brothers and sisters, and our children, who have departed this life and have by your grace been received into the place you have prepared for us, who love you and the place of your abode.

Bring us in our time to the joy and peace of heaven, through Jesus Christ our Lord, to whom with you, ageless God, and the Holy Spirit be given unending praise and glory. Amen

Fifth Sunday after the Epiphany

First Lesson - For the prophet the exalted vision leads to penitence and purging in preparation for preaching. Isaiah 6:1-8 (9-13)

Psalm 138

Second Lesson - Paul gives detailed explanation of the witnesses to the resurrection of Jesus Christ. 1 Corinthians 15:1-11

Gospel - Simon Peter like Isaiah is humbled by the awareness of a holy presence. Luke 5:1-11

CALL TO WORSHIP

Leader: The grace of our Lord Jesus Christ be with you all.
People: And also with you.
Leader: For God's love and faithfulness, let us praise God's name.
People: The promise of God is as wide as the heavens.

INVOCATION

The widest rainbow cannot span the breadth of your promises, O God, for they encompass all who will call upon your name anywhere on our planet or in our space. Your Child, Jesus, has taught us to call you Father, so we worship you in his name. Amen

PRAYER OF CONFESSION

God-in-hiding, you catch us unawares. In frightening circumstances, we find ourselves saying: "What did I do to deserve this?" In incredibly good times, we find ourselves saying, "What did I do to deserve this?" Whenever we encounter you unexpectedly, a sense of guilt may catch us, and we want you to go away. But we would rather have your forgiveness than your absence, your purging than your rejection. Forgive our sins and prepare us to serve you, through Jesus our Savior. Amen

Declaration of Pardon

Pastor: Friends, hear the Good News! You are saved by the gospel.

People: We are saved by the gospel if we hold firmly to it.

Pastor: Friends, believe the Good News!

People: In Jesus Christ, we are forgiven.

[AND]

Exhortation

Let God's grace be at work in you, drawing others into the fellowship of Christ's church.

PRAYER OF THE DAY

Urge your service on us, Lord Jesus, that we may be willing to put aside all other priorities in order to follow you. Having received your forgiveness, we accept your assignment. Amen

PRAYER OF THANKSGIVING

For visions of your glory, we give thanks, holy God; for experiences of conversion, we give thanks, holy Jesus; for confirmation and commissioning, we give thanks, Holy Spirit. For every time and place hallowed by such experiences, we declare our joyful memories. Great is your glory, O

God. Our joy in you gives us strength to do your work enabled by your grace in Jesus Christ. Amen

PRAYER OF DEDICATION

It is by your grace, Lord Jesus, that we are what we are, not all that we yet may be, but wanting to be used by you in the saving work of your church. Amen

PRAYER OF INTERCESSION AND COMMEMORATION

O God, your kingdom tarries, and we pray that your kingdom will come and your will be done on earth as it is in heaven. Help us to pray in faith according to your will.

Remember, O Lord, your church universal. Augment it in the truth of your living Word and the power of the Spirit. Make Christians of every race true partners in the ample and gracious life of your church, that they may find themselves embraced by a life mightier and holier than theirs to be nourished and to grow in grace. Inspire your church in every quarter to carry on your work of redeeming love.

Remember our country, good Lord. Maintain and prosper national leaders, granting them sound judgment, plain dealing, and the courage to do what is right in your sight.

Bless the labor of people; guard and cheer all who, in serving others, face danger for our safety or hardship for our comfort, especially miners underground, sailors and fisherfolk on the seas, and all who face hazards in their daily work.

Remember, O Lord, our children. Watch over them whether they are still at home or far away. Give them health of soul and body. Deliver them from evil. Teach them to love what is good and let them find their truest friend and kindest guide in Jesus Christ your Son.

Great Physician, hear our prayer for the sick, any who are in pain or sorrow, those who are shut in by age or infirmity. Give them a quiet spirit to rest in your strong arms, and in your good time grant them restoration and in the end eternal life.

Grant to those near death the vision of the face of Jesus Christ so that they may depart in peace according to your Word.

Eternal God, we praise you for all who have traveled with us on this pilgrim way and who have crossed over the deep river of death into the brightness of the Promised Land.

Keep us in the faith and communion of all your saints and journey with us as we complete our own pilgrimage to the Celestial City. To the ascended Christ, the everlasting Father, and the Holy Spirit be ascribed all glory and praise, now and evermore. Amen

Sixth Sunday after the Epiphany

First Lesson - Spiritual survival and growth depend on our trust in God. Jeremiah 17:5-10

Psalm 1

Second Lesson - Paul argues that denial of the resurrection of the dead undermines the whole gospel. 1 Corinthians 15:12-20

Gospel - Luke gives us his version of the Beatitudes and Woes pronounced by Jesus. Luke 6:17-26

CALL TO WORSHIP

Leader: The grace of our Lord Jesus Christ be with you all.

People: And also with you.

Leader: Come and put your confidence in God.

People: We will put our confidence in God and will not be disappointed.

INVOCATION

Trustworthy God, recall us from any bitterness and frustration in our experience with people who are not trustworthy. In our worship remind us of your promises that are positive and healing through the Spirit of Jesus Christ. Amen

PRAYER OF CONFESSION

Despite your warnings through prophets and psalmists, God of truth, we are frequently deceived by the silks and satins of palaces and cathedrals. Too often we give heed to glamorous lies rather than simple truth. We misplace our trust when we put our trust in such persons and not in you. You frequently speak through rough and ready persons like John the Baptist, heal the sick through poor people like Jesus of Nazareth, comfort the dying through servants like Mother Teresa of Calcutta. Forgive our admiration of false glories, through Jesus our Savior. Amen

Declaration of Pardon

Pastor: Friends, hear the Good News! You are blessed if you believe the Good News Jesus preaches to the poor.

People: We do not find Jesus Christ to be a stumbling block, and believe the Good News he preaches to the poor.

Pastor: Friends, believe the Good News!

People: In Jesus Christ, we are forgiven.

[AND]

Exhortation

Beware of the frivolous life. These joys soon disappear. Following Christ may not always be easy, but the rewards are enduring.

PRAYER OF THE DAY

Save us, Son of Man, Child of God, from the casual life without commitment to you, and without compassion for the sick and poor of the world. Satisfy us with that which is eternal in you, the ever-living Christ. Amen

PRAYER OF THANKSGIVING

God of the living, Christ of the resurrection, eternal Spirit, we rejoice in the survival of the church, giving thanks that the message that Christ has been raised from death has been heard and believed by many, from the time of the apostles to this day. We live in joyful belief that it is not a delusion and that we are not lost in our sins. You have vindicated the Christ in resurrection, and received him into heaven to intercede for us. Glory be to you, O God, now and always. Amen

PRAYER OF DEDICATION

Though our lives, O God, are not as fruitful as they will be, receive what we are, and what we will become, and whatever we may accomplish, by your grace in Jesus Christ. Amen

PRAYER OF INTERCESSION
AND COMMEMORATION

Eternal God, as you have bidden Israel so you also call the church of Jesus Christ to rise, shine; for your light has come, and the glory of the Lord has risen upon us. Let his glory in the church dispel the darkness that covers so much of the earth and so many of the people. Ever renew the light of the truth that is Christ by his Spirit, that nations shall come to his light and leaders to   the brightness of his dawn.

God of Israel and the church, continue to teach us in the giving of offerings the need to give ourselves as living sacrifices, holy and acceptable to you, which is our spiritual worship. Renew our minds, so that we may discern what is your will, O God—what is good and acceptable and perfect. May we live together in humility, not thinking of ourselves more highly than we ought to think.

Give to leaders in both church and state strong intelligence to think with sober judgment, each according to the measure of faith that God has assigned. Grant unified action in the church. As in one body we have many members, and not all the members have the same function, so may we exercise our various functions coordinated by the mind of Christ.

Bless all our elected officials that they may never pervert justice but govern us with respect for all people and reverence for you.

Almighty God, you made the world and named it good and gave it to our management. Make us wise enough to keep air clear and water pure and the land beautiful. Prevent us from destroying land and fouling streams. Let us treat lovely things with true appreciation so that all may enjoy the earth.

In time of need your children may come to you, O God, as to a compassionate parent. Hear the appeals of your children who are sick, or in sorrow, or fiercely tempted. Grant them help according to your wisdom and grace. Comfort the bereaved and give peace to the dying.

Eternal God, before your sight the generations rise and pass away. We rejoice for those who have left behind the toil and strife of this life for the rest and peace of eternity. Give us patience to complete our work in hope, keeping faith with your family in earth and heaven, through Jesus Christ our Lord, to whom with you and the Holy Spirit be dominion and glory, now and forever. Amen

Seventh Sunday after the Epiphany

First Lesson - Rather than blame his brothers for their ill treatment of him, Joseph shows how it is providential that he has come to a position of power that can save them from famine. Genesis 45:3-11, 15

Psalm 37:1-11, 39-40

Second Lesson - Paul's explanations of resurrection are taken from nature and Scripture. 1 Corinthians 15:35-38, 42-50

Gospel - Jesus describes the magnanimity of spirit that he expects in his disciples. Luke 6:27-38

CALL TO WORSHIP

Leader: The grace of our Lord Jesus Christ be with you all.

People: And also with you.

Leader: Be still in God's presence and worship expectantly.

People: We take delight in prayer and will receive our heart's desire.

INVOCATION

Holy God, we worship you not only in the words we say and the hymns we sing but in the silences we keep. In speaking and in listening may we be open to hear your Word and ready to respond with respectful obedience like Jesus Christ our Lord. Amen

PRAYER OF CONFESSION

Compassionate Parent, understanding Brother, loving and forgiving Spirit, you know how weak we are and how prone to retaliate when treated spitefully. We would rather return a curse with a curse and a blow with a blow. We refuse many who ask us for what we think we do not owe. We are ready to sue for the return of what is rightfully ours. How is it that you expect us to do good to those who hate us? Is it really possible that we could become so much like Jesus Christ? Forgive us, for his sake, for we are not. Amen

Declaration of Pardon

Pastor: Friends, hear the Good News! As we have worn the likeness of the human in the earth,

People: we shall wear the likeness of the heavenly one, the last Adam, Jesus Christ.

Pastor: Friends, believe the Good News!

People: In Jesus Christ, we are forgiven.

[AND]

Exhortation

Do for others just what you want them to do for you.

PRAYER OF THE DAY

How shall we be like you and your royal Son Jesus, heavenly Sovereign, unless you teach us kindness and a nobility that we rarely practice, not merely respecting our enemies, but actually loving them and praying for them as Jesus did. Amen

PRAYER OF THANKSGIVING

Life Giver, Life Sharer, Life Sustainer, many of us have experienced the nearness of death and give thanks for your restorative gifts of healing and health. We rejoice in your constant love and in the tender affection of our closest family and friends. When we have been wronged, we are happy again when justice has been brought about. Most of all we are grateful that you do not treat us as our sins deserve but with measureless forgiveness. All praise to you whose nature is life, but who in Christ Jesus shared our mortality that we might have the hope of resurrection and eternal life. Amen

PRAYER OF DEDICATION

Heavenly Monarch, your monarchy cannot be possessed by flesh and blood, nor purchased with silver and gold, but we can serve you with all that we are and have as you give us the enabling Spirit through Jesus Christ. Amen

PRAYER OF INTERCESSION
AND COMMEMORATION

Living God, you have created us as the church to be a temple for your presence. Save the church from any modern idolatry that exalts people of great gifts, in sports, in the lively arts, in the political sphere, to the pedestal of an idol. May we be the humble habitation of the Spirit, where others come to know you as their God also.

Remember for good our country's leaders and their families. Bless our nation with peace and our people with full employment.

Grant to our families a will to learn the skills of mutual support and cooperation. Make our schools laboratories of human relations skills as well as places to learn our history, develop an understanding of art and science, and grasp the obligations of citizenship.

May our place in the family of nations be assured not by military might as much as by the sharing of the best of our medical skills and humanitarian efforts in time of natural disaster. In our global village may we both teach and be taught the best of every culture. Save us from blind nationalism, racism, and religious fanaticism.

We revere your name, O God, and have seen your compassion in the face of Jesus Christ. His life is the rising sun of righteousness, and he lived among us with healing in his hands. Continue to touch with healing the sick and weak in body, mind, or spirit. Bless those who have been given healing knowledge and skill, and give wisdom and insight to those who do medical research that there may be new cures discovered for human ailments

By our common sorrows deepen our sympathies for others, and show us how to express your love to the bereaved and to those who suffer, reminding them of your suffering love in your Son, Jesus Christ.

We bless you, O God and Father of our Lord Jesus Christ, for you have blessed us in Christ with every spiritual blessing in the heavenly places, and raised us up with him and seated us with him. We rejoice in our communion with you and all whom you have taken out of the earthly struggle against evil powers into heavenly rest from strife. Bring us at last to that same unending peace and perfect community through Jesus Christ, our Savior, to whom with you and the Holy Spirit be given joyful praise. Amen

Transfiguration

First Lesson - The face of Moses is radiant with the glory of God from personal encounters to receive God's word to Israel. Exodus 34:29-35

Psalm 99

Second Lesson - Paul uses the veil over the glowing face of Moses as an illustration of failure by many to fully understand the law as leading to faith in Christ. 2 Corinthians 3:12–4:2

Gospel - On the Mount of Transfiguration the inner circle of disciples see a vision of Moses and Elijah with Jesus. Luke 9:28-36 (37-43)

CALL TO WORSHIP

Leader: The grace of our Lord Jesus Christ be with you all.

People: And also with you.

Leader: Join in the praise of the majestic name, for our mighty Sovereign is supreme over all nations.

People: We will worship with reverence before God's throne, for God is holy.

INVOCATION

Holy God, we come to honor your name with all reverence. Eternal Christ, we revere you above any prophet or human leader. Divine Spirit, we seek your aid to worship in an acceptable fashion the God who is above all description. All glory be given to you, O God. Amen

PRAYER OF CONFESSION

God of glory, God of grace, God to be seen in human face, we are not worthy of the vision of your glory and are not pure in heart to glimpse your holiness without shame. We are able to see you now as through a dark glass but anticipate the day when we will be ready to see you face to face. Extend your patience with us as we learn to love you fully and our neighbor as ourselves, through Jesus our Savior. Amen

Declaration of Pardon

Pastor: Friends, hear the Good News! God forgives us as we confess our sins.

People: Though our sins are punishable, God forgives us as we confess our sins.

Pastor: Friends, believe the Good News!

People: **In Jesus Christ, we are forgiven.**

[AND]

Exhortation

In the full light of truth live in God's sight and try to commend yourselves to everyone's good conscience.

PRAYER OF THE DAY

Revealing God, we would hear your word again so that, more brilliantly than any other memorable human beings, we enjoy the perception of Jesus as having the qualities that are those of your chosen. Amen

PRAYER OF THANKSGIVING

God of Moses and Elijah, Peter and Paul, Luther and Calvin, Pope John XXIII and Billy Graham, we give thanks for all who have revealed your word by preaching and writing. God of David and Luke, Bach and Mendelssohn, Keble and Fannie Crosby, we rejoice in the music and song that has been a means of expressing our praise to your name. God of Michaelangelo and Rembrandt, Salvador Dali and Frances Hook, we appreciate the art that has brightened our vision of your glory. Most of all we celebrate the grace you have manifest in Jesus Christ himself, seen by his generation and remembered ever since in word and sacrament. Amen

PRAYER OF DEDICATION

God of clouds and streaming light, wake us from dozing discipleship to alert witnessing and the devotion of what we are and what we have to the needs of the world in our time. Amen

PRAYER OF INTERCESSION
AND COMMEMORATION

We do not know how to pray as we ought, O God, but your Holy Spirit intercedes for us with sighs too deep for words. In turn, our Savior, Jesus Christ has taught us to pray for those who persecute us and those who abuse us. Teach us to love our enemies and show us if there are possibilities of reconciliation with them.

Bring helpful kinds of intervention in families where there is verbal, physical, and/or sexual abuse. Increase in our society the love of neighbor as one loves oneself. Help all agencies working toward the lessening of violence in our society. Protect police forces that confront the violent that they may be kept safe from injury and be careful in the use of necessary force to subdue the resisting.

Bless our legislators and judges, our ambassadors to the United Nations and other nations, and all in authority over us, that they may govern with respect to sacred law and without economic or racial or religious discrimination.

Give your angels charge over little children that they may live and play in safety. Send your church members with compassion to the sick, those in hospital, those in prison, those in shelters for the homeless.

Creator, Sustainer, and Restorer of all human life, you will never permit the righteous to be overwhelmed. You have promised that the gates of death will not prevail against the church. With confidence we put our beloved dead in your keeping and in the midst of earthly trial and temptation we cast our burden on you for you are pledged to sustain us. Uphold us evermore in time and eternity and we will ascribe to you, One God, majesty and power and glory. Amen

Lent

First Sunday in Lent

First Lesson - After the years of slavery in Egypt and the hardships of the wilderness, the people of Israel are called to celebrate the land of plenty in thanksgiving before God. Deuteronomy 26:1-11

Psalm 91:1-2, 9-16

Second Lesson - Paul assures his listeners that, whether they be Jew or Greek, there is one Lord of all. Romans 10:8b-13

Gospel - Jesus, fasting in the wilderness, overcomes the temptations of the Evil One. Luke 4:1-13

CALL TO WORSHIP

Leader: The grace of our Lord Jesus Christ be with you all.

People: And also with you.

Leader: Hear what God's Word says: I will save those who love me.

People: When we call on the Eternal One, we are answered. When we are in trouble, God will be with us.

INVOCATION

Listening God, you have been responsive to our petitions, and we come again with our prayers of adoration and thanksgiving as well as supplication. Beyond ourselves we come to pray for our families, our neighbors, our world, as our Savior Christ has taught us. Amen

PRAYER OF CONFESSION

Your name, O God, is to be spoken with reverence and hope. We have spoken it irreverently at times and not at all when we might have called upon you with expectation of your presence and help. We know you are present but put you out of our minds when we worship wealth and power. Most of us would not acknowledge ourselves devil worshipers and yet succumb to temptations that Jesus resisted with the strength of your Word. Forgive our lack of faith in your saving power or our wanting to be saved only from the consequences of our sins and not from the sins themselves, through Jesus Christ our Lord. Amen

Declaration of Pardon

Pastor: Friends, hear the Good News! Everyone who calls out to the Lord for help will be saved.

People: The scripture says, "No one who believes in him will be put to shame."

Pastor: Friends, believe the Good News!

People: In Jesus Christ, we are forgiven.

[AND]

Exhortation

Confess that Jesus is Lord. Believe that God raised him from the dead. It is by our confession that we are saved.

PRAYER OF THE DAY

God our strength, in times of need save us from despair. In times of indecision save us from opting for power rather than service. In times of danger save us from hiding rather than risking what we may do with your approval and help. We would be more like your Son, Jesus. Amen

PRAYER OF THANKSGIVING

God above history, God in our history, God at the end of history, as the ancestors of Israel were wandering Aramaeans, so our ancestors were emigrating pilgrims, seeking freedom to worship and to govern themselves according to an enlightened conscience. We are grateful for their pioneering. For all the freedoms we enjoy in this land of immigrants we give you our thanks, remembering also that we live among the remnants of those who lived here before us. We give thanks for their love of the land, the forests, and the creatures which you have created. Help us to show our thanksgiving in the continual re-examination of conscience that we may live justly, show mercy, and walk in humility before you, like Jesus Christ, your Son, our Lord. Amen

PRAYER OF DEDICATION

As your people Israel worshiped you in the presentation of the first part of the harvest, so may we your people of Christ's church worship you in the presentation of our offerings, remembering also the ministers and those of the poor in this and every land who look to us for the gifts that we share, through Jesus Christ our Lord. Amen

PRAYER OF INTERCESSION
AND COMMEMORATION

Hear, O God, our prayers on behalf of others. God of light and truth, continue to give more light to the church by the instruction of the Spirit speaking in the Word as written and as further insights are found in our communal life in the midst of a dark and evil world. Save us from being overwhelmed by the false and deceitful, that we may not be separated from the light of the world in your Son Jesus Christ, nor acknowledge any anti-Christ.

Grant salvation to those who have long known but little heeded the sound of the gospel, that finally yielding to your loving grace they may find forgiveness with you and the spirit to forgive others.

Expand the vision of all your servants. Grant certainty to those who waver in their faith, and loyalty to those who are not fully committed to serve you. So may the work of your church advance from day to day.

Bless all whom you have called to be evangelists and missionaries, that your saving word may reach those who still sit in darkness and despair.

We pray for our country and our leaders that we may live wisely, justly, and peaceably. Give us genuine concern for the needs of all, that none may go hungry or naked or homeless. Grant healing to those who are sick and assistance to those who are disabled. Give recovery to those who are distressed by addiction or other emotional anxiety.

Loving God, we rejoice in the friendships that we enjoy in the earthly communion of the church and the hope of a renewal of our most precious relationships in the peace of heaven. Keep us in your grace that we may come before you with confidence and joy. Unto you, eternal Parent, and the Prince of peace, and the Spirit of universal   presence, be ascribed all praise both now and forever. Amen

Second Sunday in Lent

First Lesson - Strange signs accompany the promise of God to Abraham concerning the magnitude of his and Sarah's posterity. Genesis 15:1-12, 17, 18

Psalm 27

Second Lesson - Paul advocates the full appreciation of dual citizenship in earth and heaven and warns against the deadliness of gluttony. Philippians 3:17–4:1

Gospel - Jesus has friends even among the party which strongly criticizes him, through whom Jesus sends a satirical message to King Herod. Luke 13:31-35
[OR]
Luke tells the story of the meeting of Jesus with two Old Testament celebrities with a testimonial from heaven to convince the inner circle of disciples as to who is greatest in the kingdom of heaven. Luke 9:28-36

CALL TO WORSHIP

Leader: The grace of our Lord Jesus Christ be with you all.

People: And also with you.

Leader: Come seek God's face; wait for the Lord; take courage; be strong.

People: We seek God's face and wait for our Lord Jesus Christ. The Spirit of Christ gives us courage and strength.

INVOCATION

Invisible God, without the incarnation of your Son, Jesus Christ, we could envision your face only vaguely. You give us the Holy Spirit to enable our prayer and our search for your truth and your will for us. In our worship strengthen us to do as well as to know your purpose for us; through Jesus Christ our Lord. Amen

PRAYER OF CONFESSION

Creating Spirit, hear our confession. We are often forgetful of who we are and in whose likeness we are created. We regret the imbalance in our lives that too often allows our appetites to run away with us, so that we seem to live for eating and drinking and love-making alone. Our minds are too to consider the refreshment of the spirit, the exercise of the mind, the discipline of the body. Forgive our excesses and deliver us from them through our Lord Jesus Christ. Amen

Declaration of Pardon

Pastor: Friends, hear the Good News! Christ will transfigure these bodies belonging to our humble state.

People: Christ will transfigure these our bodies and give them a form like that of his own resplendent body by the very power which enables him to make all things subject to himself.

Pastor: Friends, believe the Good News!
People: In Jesus Christ, we are forgiven.

[AND]

Exhortation

Live as citizens of heaven. Stand firm in the faith. Look to Jesus who will bring us joy and a crown beyond the cross.

PRAYER OF THE DAY

God of order and truth, among the many persons who appear heroic to us, help us to look only to those who remind us most vividly of Jesus of Nazareth. Help us to heed only those whose advice and guidance lead us in his ways. Speak to us through whom you please but let us never turn away from your eternal Son. Amen

PRAYER OF THANKSGIVING

Eternal God, who in Jesus Christ accepted the limitations of time as a pioneer of perseverance, we thank you for the promise that waits beyond the years of waiting, for the transformation and transfiguration that lie beyond the days of human frailty and suffering, for the light that breaks through dark clouds, and for the glory that outshines all humiliation. We are grateful for the life and suffering of Jesus and rejoice in the glory that now is his and which one day he will share with all who are willing to share his suffering; through the same Jesus Christ your Son and our Intercessor. Amen

PRAYER OF DEDICATION

In themselves our gifts are lifeless, living God, but they are a portion of our livelihood. Accept these offerings of obedient service in honor of your name and for the benefit of our neighbors in the world; through Jesus Christ our Lord. Amen

PRAYER OF INTERCESSION
AND COMMEMORATION

Generous God, you have given us a goodly heritage in your church. Grant to us new zeal and perseverance to extend your kingdom so that people everywhere by worshiping one God may be united in one holy communion of the Spirit and love for Jesus Christ your Son as their brother.

Lord Jesus Christ, you were received up into heaven and commanded your disciples to go into all the world and preach the gospel to every person. Grant your blessing to all who have responded to your command in this and every land. Hasten the day when all shall know you, honor you, and serve you, bringing glory to your name.

Gracious God, you have promised that the Christ shall not fail nor be discouraged until justice shall rule the whole earth. Save us from dishonoring your name, from strife and contention. Unite all nations in the search for peace with justice.

Keep safe all our leaders from the threat of assassins. Save them from themselves that they may not betray the trust that placed in them. When they err grant them ready repentance and renewal in their commitment to truth and justice.

Source of all life, Savior of the living, Spirit of love and truth, continue your work of healing our bodies, minds and spirits. Mend the body broken by accident, the spirit broken by sorrow, the mind that is disturbed. Strengthen the faith of those with chronic illness and grant endurance to those for whose disease there is no known cure. May all who find healing and health give thanks to you with your whole congregation.

Console those who mourn. Support the aged and infirm. Prepare the dying for the solemn change that they may greet death in hope of your grace and at peace with their family and neighbors.

We give thanks for all your people who have lived and died in the faith of Jesus and especially for those who were closest to us and who worshiped with us in your house of prayer here or elsewhere. We rejoice in the happiness they now enjoy and anticipate by your grace that we may also be freed from all evil and join them in your eternal home.

Hear, O God, these our thanksgivings and intercessions, which we bring in the name of your Son, Jesus Christ, to whom with you and the Holy Spirit be all glory, time without end. Amen

Third Sunday in Lent

First Lesson - The prophet makes an eloquent appeal, offering a spiritual banquet of food and drink as the outcome of repentance. Isaiah 55:1-9

Psalm 63:1-8

Second Lesson - Paul warns the Corinthians that sexual immorality can be a deadly sin. 1 Corinthians 10:1-13

Gospel - The relatively innocent may suffer with the guilty, but the day of judgment will come for everyone in due course, warns Jesus. Luke 13:1-9

CALL TO WORSHIP

Leader: The grace of our Lord Jesus Christ be with you all.

People: And also with you.

Leader: Seek the Eternal One who may be found. Call upon God while the Spirit is near.

People: We will forsake wicked ways and unrighteous thoughts. We will return to the Eternal One, who will have mercy on us, and to our God, who will abundantly pardon.

INVOCATION

Eternal God, we return to your house to pray, and we turn from sinful ways at your bidding. We rejoice in your promised pardon and seek to fill our minds with the high ideals of your holy Word as written by prophets and apostles and lived out in Jesus Christ. Amen

PRAYER OF CONFESSION

Holy God, how exalted are your ways! Holy Savior, how sinless is your life! Holy Spirit, how pure is your nature! Whatever progress we have made along the road of righteousness we are far behind the advance of your Son Jesus. Continue to call us back when we go off on a tangent and recall us to the upward way, for we would more nearly follow Jesus Christ. Amen

Declaration of Pardon

Pastor: Friends, hear the Good News! God comes to free us from slavery to every passion.

People: God is faithful and will not let us be tested beyond our strength.

Pastor: Friends, believe the Good News!

People: In Jesus Christ, we are forgiven.

[AND]

Exhortation

Repent. God is patient but looks for the fruits of repentance.

PRAYER OF THE DAY

Save us, God of the living, from any misconception that because we survive and others meet untimely deaths, that we are more virtuous than they. Whether our lives are long or short may they be truly fruitful through the Spirit of Jesus Christ. Amen

PRAYER OF THANKSGIVING

God of order, God of compassion, God of love, we rejoice that catastrophes are as infrequent as they are. Even then you inspire mutual helpfulness among those who suffer from them as well as those near enough to lend a hand. We are grateful that we have learned how to avoid some of the violence that is part of nature, and we are committed to caring for your creation with all the wisdom you will give us in experience. We praise your wisdom, power, and glory through Jesus Christ our Lord. Amen

PRAYER OF DEDICATION

Receive the offerings we bring, O God, and sanctify them to the holy purpose of proffering your spiritual gifts to all who desire them; through Jesus Christ our Lord. Amen

PRAYER OF INTERCESSION
AND COMMEMORATION

God of all, hear our prayers in the name of Jesus Christ. Bless your church and refine your people to be the salt of the earth. May our children also, cleansed by water and the Spirit, help to purify the life of our society.

Unite all who honor the name of Jesus and make the church strong in its witness to his grace offered to all who will receive his salvation from their sins. May the love you have for the hungry be met by feeding programs, the need for housing be served by programs like Habitat for Humanity, the shortage of doctors and healers be met by clinics established by the church where they are most needed.

Hear our prayers for our country and our leaders. Keep them safe and well, ready to guide us in paths of peace and goodness. Teach all of us tolerance for those who seem too different from us, and give us true consideration for the freedom of all. Give zeal and wisdom to all who can increase employment and those seeking justice for others who have been wronged, oppressed, or defrauded of their rightful earnings.

Heal the sick. Cheer the sad. Relieve the   anxious. Give peace of mind to those who are disturbed. Free those who are addicted to alcohol or other drugs and powerless without your help.

Eternal God, we rejoice in your gracious gathering of a great and blessed company who have inherited your promises and give thanks for the companions of our life's journey who have already reached their destination with you. May we complete our sojourn without despair and full of hope in the fulfillment of our salvation by the mercy of Jesus.

Christ, to whom with you and the Holy Spirit be glory and praise, time without end. Amen

Fourth Sunday in Lent

First Lesson - Gilgal becomes a memorable place for the former slaves who can celebrate the Passover outside the land of their prior captivity. Joshua 5:9-12

Psalm 32

Second Lesson - Jesus the non-sinner is made to be sin in order that we sinners might be reconciled to God and become Christian representatives of the new creation. 2 Corinthians 5:16-21

Gospel - The parables of Jesus are purposeful in answering the complaints of his critics. Luke 15:1-3, 11b-32

CALL TO WORSHIP

Leader: The grace of our Lord Jesus Christ be with you all.
People: And also with you.
Leader: Be glad in the Lord and rejoice, O righteous,

People: We shout for joy for our heart is in the right place.

INVOCATION

Holy, Holy, Holy God, we are righteous only as you see us in the likeness of Jesus Christ your perfect Child and our brother. Receive the worship we offer you in his name. Amen

PRAYER OF CONFESSION

Generous and forgiving Parent, we are not sinless like your Son, Jesus of Nazareth. We confess our misdeeds knowing that you have reconciled us to yourself through the identification of the Sinless One with us in our sinfulness. Though we are not worthy to be called your children and deserve to be treated only as servants of earlier times, we come with confidence in your generosity. If we continue in sin, presuming on your forgiveness, mercifully withhold the judgment we have coming to us, for the sake of Jesus Christ. Amen

Declaration of Pardon

Pastor: Friends, hear the Good News! When anyone is united to Christ, there is a new world.

People: The old order has gone, and a new order has already begun.

Pastor: Friends, believe the Good News!

People: In Jesus Christ, we are forgiven.

[AND]

Exhortation

Celebrate with God the return of every lost and wandering child who returns to the way and to the family of God.

PRAYER OF THE DAY

Gracious Parent, fill our hearts with such true appreciation of your grace from day to day, that we may avoid self-righteousness and join in the joyful celebration of the recovery and return of other prodigals through Jesus Christ, who came to seek and to save all who are lost. Amen

PRAYER OF THANKSGIVING

Though we might well hang our heads in shame, heavenly Parent, when we remember what we have done contrary to your instruction, we come with joy and shining faces, for you put our past behind us and lead us to a new life of freedom and mutual service. We will bless your name continually and tell of your goodness to the humble, who will hear and also be glad. With all who have been freed from bondage we celebrate the Passover of gladness and the joyful feast of the people of God. All praise be given to you, holy Parent, innocent Kin, family Spirit. Amen

PRAYER OF DEDICATION

You give us more than we deserve, Divine Provider. What we give is not all that we have, but we are determined to do our best.

PRAYER OF INTERCESSION AND COMMEMORATION

Unless the Lord builds the house, those who build it labor in vain. Save us from futile efforts, O God, that accomplish nothing in building up your church. May our continuing search for truth unite us in our obedience to you. May your loving Spirit enlarge our openness to others whom you would embrace in forgiveness and renewal of life. Save us from confusing prejudice with truth so that contention will be lessened and humility bring peace. Uphold all whom you have ordained to the ministry of word and sacrament and elders and deacons and all officers in your church that their private life and public service may honor your name.

Bless and defend our country and our leaders at every level of government. May truth and justice be established among us, good manners and customs be maintained, wickedness curbed, your laws observed, and true religion increased.

We pray for all who find themselves in times of difficulty and distress of body, mind, or spirit, especially those near and dear to us whom we name in the silence before you. Though we do not merit your blessing, for the sake of Christ grant healing, patience, and peace to all who look to you in faith.

Dying and rising Savior, send your Comforter to all who are dying that they may commend themselves to the everlasting arms in hope of resurrection to eternal life.

God of the living, in this life and the next, we are grateful that you are preparing a place for all who love you. We rejoice that we are surrounded with a great cloud of witnesses, those who have finished their course and   entered into the place of triumph and rest. May we continue to hand on the Good News we have received from them and at the last share their triumph; through Jesus Christ, who lives and reigns with you and the Holy Spirit, one God, time without end. Amen

Fifth Sunday in Lent

First Lesson - The prophet cites past achievements of God on behalf of Israel as signs of hope for new things yet to come. Isaiah 43:16-21

Psalm 126

Second Lesson - Paul as well as the prophet wants us to look ahead and reach ahead toward goals not yet reached. Philippians 3:4b-14

Gospel - The death of Jesus is imminent and his body is anointed with a costly perfume as a sign of love by Mary. John 12:1-8

CALL TO WORSHIP

Leader: The grace of our Lord Jesus Christ be with you all.

People: And also with you.

Leader: Worship in expectation that God will do new things

People: that now they may break from the bud into flowers and fruit.

INVOCATION

God unchanging, we are assured of your steadfast love and continuing attention. Hear our praise, our confessions, our petitions, our thanksgivings and intercessions through your Son, Jesus Christ, and the communion of the Holy Spirit. Amen

PRAYER OF CONFESSION

God for all seasons, we confess that we would rather live in the glorious days of the past than risk the uncertain outcome of the future. We would rather leap ahead to the day of resurrection than undergo our share of the sufferings of Christ. Forgive our zeal for honors and our reluctance to accept either unnoticed service or too-conspicuous suffering, through Jesus Christ, who through humiliation came to exaltation. Amen

Declaration of Pardon

Pastor: Friends, hear the Good News! With the twelve we are invited to eat and drink at our Lord's Table in the kingdom of God.

People: From east and west, from north and south, we gather together at the Lord's Table.

Pastor: Friends, believe the Good News!

People: In Jesus Christ, we are forgiven.

[AND]

Exhortation

Forget what is behind and press on to the goal. There you will win the prize, which is God's call to the life above with Christ Jesus.

PRAYER OF THE DAY

Suffering Servant, triumphant Lord, strengthen our resolve to serve you faithfully at the humblest tasks so that we may be prepared for whatever duties you will assign us in the kingdom yet to come, through the power of your resurrection. Amen

PRAYER OF THANKSGIVING

We bless you, O Lord, for you have heard our cries for mercy. You are our strength and shield, and we trust you with all our hearts. You sustain us, and our hearts leap up for joy. We praise you with our whole bodies. You are the strength of your people. Without you we cannot hope to complete the race and win the prize. We rejoice in your promised presence with us, now and always. Amen

PRAYER OF DEDICATION

Receive the faithful service of your church, risen Lord, as we maintain your table and celebrate your supper here in anticipation of the final fulfillment of this Passover in the kingdom of God. Amen

PRAYER OF INTERCESSION
AND COMMEMORATION

Sovereign God, we pray for all humanity that your ways may be known to all and your saving health in all nations.

We pray that your whole church, filled with the Spirit, may be a light everywhere and a shelter and sanctuary for those threatened by trouble and violence. May we be known for our mercy and tender love and care for the hurting and helpless. Keep us in the truth, holding the mystery of the faith in a good conscience, in love which is the bond of peace, and in all godliness of life.

We pray for all our national leaders who confess the Christian faith that their integrity may be an example not only to the people but to other leaders who make no such confession. Bless all who lead us that their plans may be well and truly made as in your sight, and executed impartially as under your judgment, that all may know justice and honor be given to your name.

We pray for all schools, public and private, colleges and universities. Bless students and teachers at every level that no gifts may be neglected or talents spoiled. Guide those who do research that they may find and invent what is constructive and healthful to the good of people and your glory.

To your healing care we commend all who are distressed in body, mind, or spirit, especially those young or old, known and dear to us, whom we remember before you in our hearts. Comfort, heal, and relieve them as they have need, giving them patience in their trials, and in your time a happy end to their troubles.

Shepherd of our souls, we rejoice in the communion of saints, for the awareness in heaven of the struggles on earth and for the sweet memory of those our beloved who have entered into ultimate peace. Let your goodness and mercy follow us all our days that we may dwell in your house forever and give eternal praise to you, fatherly, brotherly, motherly God, One God, forever. Amen

Sixth Sunday in Lent

First Lesson - The suffering servant shares his experience of resignation and trust in God who will vindicate him at last. Isaiah 50:4-9a

†**Psalm** 118:1-2, 19-29 (As Palm Sunday)

††**Psalm** 31:9-16 (As Passion Sunday)

Second Lesson - Paul urges humility and cooperation with the divine purpose rather than stubbornness and prideful opposition. Philippians 2:5-11

†**Gospel** - The Messiah who is humble and obedient to the divine plan is not diverted by either praise or opposition. Luke 19:28-40

††**Gospel** - The hours of our Lord's deepest sufferings are chronicled by Luke. Luke 22:14–23:56
[OR]
Luke 23:1-49

†CALL TO WORSHIP

Leader: The grace of our Lord Jesus Christ be with you all.
People: And also with you.
Leader: Reverence the name of the Lord in the evening
People: and his glory to the rising of the sun.

††CALL TO WORSHIP

Leader: The grace of our Lord Jesus Christ be with you all.
People: And also with you.
Leader: Listen again for the Word of God.
**People: Morning by morning God wakens us—wakens us
    to listen as those who are taught.**

†INVOCATION

In public worship and in private devotion we hallow your name, God of creation, Christ of the cross, Spirit of love. Be present to us as we have heeded again your invitation to celebrate your gracious actions in Jesus Christ our Savior. Amen

††INVOCATION

Gracious God, give this preacher, like the prophet, the tongue of a teacher, that he may know how to sustain the weary with a word, your Word, written by inspiration and lived by incarnation; through Jesus Christ our Lord. Amen

†PRAYER OF CONFESSION

God of justice, you still look for those who love justice and practice honesty in business and in court. Too often you look in vain for those who will intervene in opposition to injustice and those who will tell the truth without any equivocation. Too often we are cowardly and turn our backs on those who need our advocacy in the cause of freedom with justice. Forgive any compromise of integrity and any indifference to miscarriages of justice. Have mercy on us for the sake of Jesus Christ, your suffering servant and our Savior. Amen

††PRAYER OF CONFESSION

Sympathetic Parent, Suffering Servant, Consoling Spirit, forgive our apathy in the face of your identification with our sins. We are still so insensitive to the abhorrence you have to all evil. Despite your holiness you forgive our sins both deliberate and unknowing. Hear us as in the silence we bring to mind our more obvious sins. Only in the name of Jesus do we have assurance of pardon and any disposition to examine ourselves more deeply.

†Declaration of Pardon

Pastor: Friends, hear the Good News! When it is the Lord God who helps you,

People: who will declare you guilty?

Pastor: Friends, believe the Good News!

People: In Jesus Christ, we are forgiven.

[AND]

†Exhortation

Deal mercifully with others, displaying the patience God can give. Be typical of all who in the future will also have faith in Christ and gain eternal life.

††Declaration of Pardon

Pastor: Friends, hear the Good News! Hear the words of Jesus even now being said for us:

People: "Father, forgive them for they know not what they do."

Pastor: Friends, believe the Good News!

People: In Jesus Christ, we are forgiven.

[AND]

††Exhortation

In life and in death commit your lives into the hands of God.

†PRAYER OF THE DAY

Modest King, receive our praise for all that you do for us from day to day. We would speak and sing in harmony with all of nature that glorifies you, God of grace. Amen

††PRAYER OF THE DAY

Sensitizing Spirit, open our hearts to the suffering that our sins add to the suffering of God's chosen One, so that we may be deterred from displeasing our heavenly Parent and desire the purity of holy childhood. Amen

†PRAYER OF THANKSGIVING

We rejoice, O God, in your steadfastness. When life is uncertain, you are a rock of refuge. When friends are ashamed of us, you are still merciful and forgiving. How abundant is your goodness beyond all deserving! Your look of love and encouragement we see in the face of Jesus Christ. You see us through places of affliction and set our feet again in a safe place. We praise your name, Creator, Healer, Sustainer. Amen

††PRAYER OF THANKSGIVING

Loving God, crucified Christ, living Spirit, to what lengths you go to manifest your caring for sinners, that Jesus should be counted a criminal to be identified with us all. To what depths you have come from the majesty of heaven to servitude and suffering, humility and mortality. We rejoice in the glory that now you share again, risen Messiah, having borne out sorrow, you have entered into joy. We live in thankful expectation of sharing that eternal happiness because of your indescribable self-sacrifice. We give thanks to you, Giver of all good gifts. We give thanks to you, God-given Jesus. We give thanks to you, still-given Spirit. Amen

††PRAYER OF DEDICATION

Source of all goodness, the temporal value of the offerings we bring varies with the marketplace, but the eternal value of your church's work remains constant as you enable us to serve you in the power of the Spirit. Evermore give us abounding grace through Jesus Christ our Lord. Amen

††PRAYER OF DEDICATION

No gift of ours can match the gift you have given us in Christ, giving God, but our offerings are an expression of our need to serve you, faithfully and humbly. Amen

PRAYER OF INTERCESSION
AND COMMEMORATION

Universal God, you have commanded us to pray for all humanity, so we pray for all nations and peoples, that all who are still groping after you may find you through Jesus Christ our Lord.

Cleanse and sanctify your church, the living temple of the Holy Spirit that it may truly be a house of prayer for many nations and all kinds of people. Hasten the day when the kingdoms of this world become the kingdom of our Lord and his Christ. Overturn and overrule ungodly governments until he comes whose right it is to rule the world that he saves by his death and resurrection.

God of our ancestors and our children, without the church planting of our ancestors we would have no place of prayer, and without children in the faith the church will not survive. Continue to teach us the faith that we may celebrate your grace in the sacraments and hand on the traditions of the church to another faithful generation.

Keep in your rule and care our national leaders that good government may be found throughout our country and our relations with other nations be everywhere based on peace with justice.

Bless all business and industry that there may be work for all who need it and a fair share of the good things you have created for all people to enjoy.

Remember in your mercy the poor and needy, the unemployed and the disabled, widows and widowers, orphans and abandoned children. Comfort those who mourn.

Bless the sick and the dying, especially those known to us. Relieve their needs, console the sorrowful, heal the sick, and in due time lift them up to give thanksgiving in the congregation.

Bishop of our souls, we join in thanksgiving with the hosts of your saints who in bright array and with palms of victory have entered the gates of your Holy City. Grant us strength to follow them as they followed Christ that at the end of our earthly life by the triumph of Christ we may mount up to the life of heaven and be forever with the Lord.

These our thanksgivings and prayers we offer to you, Father eternal, through Jesus Christ your Son, who lives and reigns and is worshiped and glorified with the mothering Spirit, one God, time without end. Amen

*E*aster

Easter

First Lesson - Here is an early outline of Peter's sermon, the heart of the Gospel which will be preached to the ends of the earth. Acts 10:34-43

Psalm 118:1-2, 14-24

Second Lesson - The Apostle makes it clear that the resurrection of Jesus to life after death is the heart of Christian faith. 1 Corinthians 15:19-26 [or Acts 10:34-43]

Gospel - The dearest friends of Jesus discover the empty tomb and Mary Magdalene actually meets the risen Christ. John 20:1-18
[OR]
Luke accounts for beginning of the Christian celebration of the first day of the week as the day of resurrection. Luke 24:1-12

CALL TO WORSHIP

Leader: The grace of our Lord Jesus Christ be with you all.
People: And also with you.
Leader: This is the day of the Lord's victory.
People: We will celebrate and be happy.

INVOCATION

Glorious God, we celebrate the new day not only as the rising of the sun after the darkness of the night, but as the rising of your Son Jesus after the darkness of the valley of the shadow of death. All glory be given to you: living God, risen Christ, eternal Spirit. Amen

PRAYER OF CONFESSION

God without favorites, we confess that we have our preferences according to nationality and custom. We do not easily

86

accept religious practices other than our own. We find it difficult to discern the similarities below the surface differences and the deeper reverence for you that we may share. We need to learn to witness to our faith in you without pride of race and nationality. Forgive any exclusive attitude that may prevent our communicating the Good News of the resurrection of our dying, rising, living Savior, Jesus Christ. Amen

Declaration of Pardon

Pastor: Friends, hear the Good News! The Lord's love endures forever.

People: The Lord chastens us but does not surrender us to death. He is our deliverer.

Pastor: Friends, believe the Good News!

People: In Jesus Christ, we are forgiven.

[AND]

Exhortation

Like Mary Magdalene, go to tell the family of Jesus that he is risen and ascends to his God and ours.

PRAYER OF THE DAY

Eternal God, grant us time to discover in our own experience the meaning of your written Word so that the One who is your   Word spelled out in our humanity will inform our minds and transform our personalities in the Spirit of Jesus Christ. Amen

PRAYER OF THANKSGIVING

You are no grim reaper, Creator of life and Sovereign of death, but a joyful Harvester. We rejoice in the resurrection of Jesus who is the firstfruits of the harvest of the dead. We may live in happy anticipation of our own life beyond death, assured that as in Adam all die, so in Christ all will be brought to life again in your time and place. Thanks to you, our Creator, our Restorer, our Life. Amen

PRAYER OF DEDICATION

God of the living, not only in one great hour of sharing, but in all the days of our lives, use us and our total resources to help feed the hungry, to heal the sick, to bring good news to the despondent, through Jesus Christ, our risen Lord. Amen

PRAYER OF INTERCESSION AND COMMEMORATION

God of power and might, you have taught us to pray also for others as for ourselves. Hear our humble intercessions for our brothers and sisters in the world family of your creation.

Give power to your church more and more to exalt the name of Jesus in works of faith, hope, and love. Hasten the time when at the name that is above every name, at the name of Jesus, every knee should bend, in heaven and on earth and under the earth, and every tongue should confess that Jesus Christ is Lord, to the glory of God the Father. Grant to your church a singing spirit and a clear and simple witness before the world for the truth and grace in Christ Jesus.

Bless our nation's leaders and those who advise them, that they and all who serve in various capacities and at different levels of government may be cleansed of all scandalous and hurtful things. Bring to places of authority those who would increase purity, sobriety, fair dealing, and kindness among all of us.

Merciful God, we pray for all who at this stage of life are in ill health or suffering from accident or the ravages of age. Cheer, heal, and bless the sick and disabled.

Give us Easter faith that when we bid farewell at the passing of those closest to us, we may do so with confidence, at peace with them and with you. And when our day of departure comes may we follow with joy the procession that has preceded us.

We commemorate with thanksgiving the faithful and blessed departed and give thanks for all who by death have passed into life eternal. As we rejoice in their beatitude may their example inspire our ongoing life that we may live worthily in the communion of the church, to the glory of your name, Father of glory, Son of God/Son of Mary, motherly Spirit, one God, blessed for ever. Amen

Second Sunday of Easter

First Lesson - The stubborn refusal of the apostles to desist in the speading of the Good News in Jerusalem brings examination before the council. Acts 5:27-32

Psalm 118:14-29
[OR]
Psalm 150

Second Lesson - To Christians in a period of persecution John brings visions of the risen Lord in glory. Revelation 1:4-8

Gospel - The risen Christ appears to his disciples first in the absence of Thomas, then with the questioner present. John 20:19-31

CALL TO WORSHIP

Leader: The grace of our Lord Jesus Christ be with you all.

People: And also with you.

Leader: Worship reverently the One who is, who was, and who is to come, Sovereign of sovereigns.

People: We will worship together with the faithful witness, the first-born from the dead, Jesus, our high priest.

INVOCATION

Heavenly Sovereign, we approach your throne with awe, but in the company of your Son, Jesus Christ, who speaks for us as our high priest. Receive our worship inspired by the Spirit for the sake of the first-born from the dead, our living Lord, Jesus Christ. Amen

PRAYER OF CONFESSION

Alpha God, Omega God, you are our beginning and our end. We confess that we are reluctant to be counted among those responsible for the crucifixion of the One you sent to be our Savior. We may be doubtful too about the testimony to his resurrection. Forgive the pride that prevents our honest confession of sin and the doubt that refuses to hear and see what might strengthen our wavering faith. Despite our reservations, we pray in the name of your special Son, Jesus of Nazareth, your anointed One, our Savior. Amen

Declaration of Pardon

Pastor: Friends, hear the Good News! Jesus is alive and holds the keys of death and death's domain.

People: Jesus is the first and the last and is the living One. He is forgiving and says: Do not be afraid.

Pastor: Friends, believe the Good News!

People: In Jesus Christ, we are forgiven.

[AND]

Exhortation

Exult in the triumph of Jesus over death. He makes us a royal priesthood to bring others to God.

PRAYER OF THE DAY

Come to us, immortal Monarch, in the time of our doubting to reassure us, that as you were vulnerable but victorious in the circumstances of history you will bring us safely through all testing to final triumph. Amen

PRAYER OF THANKSGIVING

Living Spirit, we give thanks for all that has been recorded in the gospels of all that Jesus performed in the presence of the apostles. We rejoice in the other signs too numerous to be written that Christ has given among your people, then and now: the healing of the sick, the peace that has been given to those who have been doubtful but wanting to believe. We exult in the fellowship of the risen Monarch and live in hope of the final triumph of your rule. Amen

PRAYER OF DEDICATION

We offer to you, O God, these tangible gifts, daily work, the hymns that we sing, the music that we make, the deeds of kindness done for others, the words of encouragement spoken in your name. Receive and sanctify our gifts to extend the power of your realm to the glory of Jesus Christ, your resurrected Son. Amen

PRAYER OF INTERCESSION
AND COMMEMORATION

God of perfection, you condescend to work through imperfect human beings to unify and perfect your church. May we never rest content with divisions nor acquiesce with contentions that jeopardize the unity of the church for which Christ prayed. As there are many members but one body, may the one Spirit be obeyed who is at work in us to bring us into increasingly apparent unity so that all people may know that you have sent the Christ to be the Savior of the world and be drawn to him whom you sent to be lifted up on the cross and raised again from the dead. Though the church may be as wounded as the earthly body of the crucified, may it know the power of his resurrection and the healing and wholeness of your Holy Spirit.

Incline our leaders' hearts to seek your honor in the promotion of the peace and prosperity of the nation. Preserve the best of our origins but free us from old prejudices that excluded women as persons with equal political privilege and ignored slaves as non-persons. Strengthen us in the purpose to provide true liberty and justice for all not only for our sakes but as a light of freedom to the whole world.

Creator and Sustainer of life, continue to give us our daily bread so that we may have health and strength to do what is good and after our work enjoy an interval of rest. On our day of rest renew us in body, mind, and spirit, so that we may return to our daily vocation with renewed vigor.

We pray for all who live in a difficult time. Grant recovery to the sick, consolation to the bereaved, calm to the anxious, courage to the tempted, and victory to the embattled; through Jesus Christ our Lord.

Eternal God, we praise your name for the great company of the saints in glory, for your apostles, prophets, martyrs, and confessors, the light of the church in every age of history and especially for our own dear saints who have gone home to you. As we keep alive their memory may we live more worthy of their communion in which we may abide both now and forever. To you, O God, Ancient of Days, Brother of all generations, ageless Spirit, one God, be ascribed all honor and glory time without end. Amen

Third Sunday of Easter

First Lesson - The remarkable conversion of Saul will create the Paul who becomes a great emissary of the gospel. Acts 9:1-6 (7-20)

Psalm 30

Second Lesson - The Lamb of God slain for the sins of the world is here envisioned as triumphant in glory. Revelation 5:11-14

Gospel - Peter, who has three times denied his connection with Jesus under duress, now is admonished three times in the duties of his apostolate. John 21:1-19

CALL TO WORSHIP

Leader: The grace of our Lord Jesus Christ be with you all.

People: And also with you.

Leader: Sing a psalm to our God, all loyal servants.

People: We will give thanks and hallow God's name.

INVOCATION

God of holiness and peace, grant us an honest spirit in our worship that we may get beyond the disquiet of your hatred of sin to the forgiveness you grant to the penitent; through Jesus Christ our Lord. Amen

PRAYER OF CONFESSION

God of every tribe and language, people and nation, your dying, rising Son is the Lamb of God who comes to take away the sins of the world. We are sinners, too, thinking first of ourselves, taking whatever we can get, giving as little as possible, being more critical of others than of ourselves, slow to forgive and to seek forgiveness. Forgive our resistance to your Holy Spirit, who is ready to help us to be obedient in deed and word, for the sake of Jesus Christ, our Savior. Amen

Declaration of Pardon

Pastor: Friends, hear the Good News! God has raised Jesus from the death of the cross and has exalted him as our leader and Savior.

People: Our Savior grants us repentance and forgiveness of sins.

Pastor: Friends, believe the Good News!

People: In Jesus Christ, we are forgiven.

[AND]

Exhortation

Be witnesses to all this. The Holy Spirit is given to those who are obedient to him. Love him more than all else.

PRAYER OF THE DAY

Living Christ, meet us at the place of our daily work so that what we do may be done with patience and honesty and be offered to you as our obedient service. Amen

PRAYER OF THANKSGIVING

Worthy is the Lamb that was slain to receive all power and wealth, wisdom and might, honor and glory and praise. You have purchased us at the cost of your own blood to be members of your royal house, to serve as priests in your church, to bring your rule to this disordered earth. We rejoice in your grace that includes us in the plan to reclaim and redeem the world. Amen

PRAYER OF DEDICATION

We offer to you our prayers, our songs, our offerings, that this service may be the means of caring for the flock of the Good Shepherd who laid down his life for his sheep, Jesus Christ our Lord. Amen

PRAYER OF INTERCESSION AND COMMEMORATION

Loving Creator of all humanity, hear our prayers for all whom you love and for whom you sent your Son as the Light of the world. Dispel the gross darkness still to be found in the earth. Destroy every godless and oppressive power and bind the nations in justice and peace. Look favorably upon our nation and its leaders. Save them from the love of power that leads to self-worship and gross pride. Give wisdom to all branches of government establishing among them pure purpose, impartial judgment, and sound speech that cannot be condemned. Subdue covetousness and spread among all people a contentment with what is fair and pleasure in doing your will.

Bless this county where we live: its magistrates and police, doctors and nurses, teachers and preachers, farmers and merchants, and all who work at home and elsewhere. Cleanse our life from corruption and crime. Educate young and old that ignorance and prejudice may become things of the past. Bless our clinics and hospitals that suffering may be relieved and diseases healed. Increase opportunities for employment and respect for property and personal rights. Bless every agency that works for the relief of the poor and the sick.

Be present to the prayers of the sick, the thoughts of the distressed in mind, the anxious in their struggle against adversity. Especially be with our families and friends who may be in times of trial, that they may be comforted, healed and delivered.

Bless, O God, your church in the world that its unity and holiness may be more clearly manifest to all people. May leaders and people alike be steadfast in their witness to the truth, tolerant to the ignorant and those without understanding. May your church offer graciously the forgiveness already experienced from you, that sinners may be cleansed, doubters brought to faith, and wanderers welcomed home to the church.

Lord of all life, we praise and thank you for all our companions in the faith who have finished their time of earthly service, who now serve you beyond our sight. Grant that we may continue to live this present life as their heirs in grace, accepting responsibilities they have   left for us to fulfill. Finally, reunite us all in your heavenly service when hope will give way to sight and we serve you face to face in all humility and love. To you, holy God, fatherly, brotherly, motherly, one God, be ascribed all wisdom, and love, and perfection, now and forever. Amen

Fourth Sunday of Easter

First Lesson - A remarkable healing gives us the names of an early church member known for her good works and acts of charity. Acts 9:36-43

Psalm 23

Second Lesson - John sees vision after vision of triumph and hope for those who have been persecuted and martyred for the faith. Revelation 7:9-17

Gospel - Jesus pictures himself as shepherding all who believe that he has been sent to do the work of God. John 10:22-30

CALL TO WORSHIP

Leader: The grace of our Lord Jesus Christ be with you all.

People: And also with you.

Leader: The Lord has prepared a table before us in his house.

People: We are invited to dwell in the house of the Lord our whole life long.

INVOCATION

Heavenly Shepherd and Bishop of our souls, your goodness and mercy follow us all our days. We are grateful that you have gathered us in your fold and that in this sanctuary we are safe in your care. Hear the prayers we offer to you for your own name's sake. Amen

PRAYER OF CONFESSION

God our Savior, you have promised us eternal life for following the Good Shepherd your Son, Jesus Christ. In the confidence that you will not let us perish, we acknowledge that we are not worthy of your care and do not follow Jesus as nearly as we should. Forgive our sins for his sake that we may rejoice with all angels and martyrs around your heavenly throne, for "salvation belongs to our God who sits upon the throne, and to the Lamb." Amen

Declaration of Pardon

Pastor: Friends, hear the Good News! Jesus gives us eternal life.

People: Jesus promises that we will be his forever.

Pastor: Friends, believe the Good News!

People: In Jesus Christ, we are forgiven.

[AND]

Exhortation

Trust the Good Shepherd to lead you, and do not look for your own way.

PRAYER OF THE DAY

Give us courage, O Christ, to speak boldly in your name, whether your word is reviled or believed. Wherever we are, let your light and love shine through us so that your salvation may be brought to every locality by your Spirit within us. Amen

PRAYER OF THANKSGIVING

God beyond all time and place, God within all times and places, God eternal and universal, blessing and glory and power and might be given to you through timeless ages. We rejoice in the hope of peace beyond times of trouble, of plenty beyond hunger and thirst, of the end of sin and grief through your cleansing and consolation. We praise the tenderness with which you wipe every tear from the eyes of those who have come through great trouble. We are as moved by your gentleness as by your glory in Jesus Christ, your healing and humble Son. Amen

PRAYER OF DEDICATION

On this first day of the week, O Christ, we make our offerings with people of thousands of languages and many cultural differences. You set one table in the midst of us. Draw us close to each other whenever we approach your table. Amen

PRAYER OF INTERCESSION
AND COMMEMORATION

Just and holy God, hear our intercessions at your mercy seat through our only mediator, Jesus Christ.

Hear our prayers for all your people in the church that all the faithful under the guidance of the Holy Spirit may advance in the teaching of Jesus and the way of the cross. Gather the church from all nations into one holy communion confessing one Lord, one faith, one baptism, that Christ may be glorified. Hasten the promised day when all human cultures shall present their diverse gifts at the throne of your royal Son Jesus.

Hear our prayers for all who make our laws and exercise authority over us as for the whole citizenry of our nation. Inform our opinions and influence our voting. Spread an ardor for virtuous living without self-righteousness and merciless judgment of others. Increase among us pure religion that exalts you and cares for all whom you love.

Hear our prayers for the distressed and those beset with difficulty, embittered by loss or deceived by false values, and for all who are shaken in faith or broken in spirit.

For the sick and those worn down by chronic illness; for all who have been hurt by accident or are victims of violence; for those deprived of sight, hearing, or speech; for those who are deranged and those who cannot learn; for all who mourn and for those near to death; for all who desire our prayers, but whose need we do not know or have forgotten; for all these, hear our prayer, O God. Come to our aid in your mercy to heal and comfort that we may serve you more fully.

Lord of life and glory, we praise and bless you for all your saints who served your will in their day and generation and have now entered into rest. We bless you for our own beloved dead who have gone before us in patient hope and persevered in the way of Christ. Grant us grace like them to be faithful unto death so that at the last we too may enter into unutterable joy.

Glory and honor and dominion and power be unto our God, for ever and ever. Amen

Fifth Sunday of Easter

First Lesson - A mysterious vision opens Peter's heart to include Gentiles in the church. Acts 11·1-18

Psalm 148

Second Lesson - John describes a vision of the new heaven and earth: the New Jerusalem. Revelation 21:1-6

Gospel - Jesus says that the distinguishing feature of his disciples should be their love for one another. John 13:31-35

CALL TO WORSHIP

Leader: The grace of our Lord Jesus Christ be with you all.
People: And also with you.
Leader: Praise the name of the Eternal One,
People: for God's name alone is exalted.

INVOCATION

Glorious God, by resurrection you empower the crucified Christ and also the witness of the church. Your Spirit enables us in worship as in service to the world. Only in the Spirit may we seek and find you, who has sought and found us; through Jesus Christ our Lord. Amen

PRAYER OF CONFESSION

God of hope, you promise to make all things new, to make a new heaven and a new earth. You have been patient in your desire to restore your world to its original perfection. You have shown great forbearance to belligerent and stubborn humanity. Forgive our unwillingness to be changed, to be open to others, to open the doors of the church to those quite different from ourselves. We are sorry for the petty quarrels that spoil the resemblance the church should have to a warm and loving family. Continue your patience with us until we are mature in your love and peace, through Jesus Christ our Lord. Amen

Declaration of Pardon

Pastor: Friends, hear the Good News! We are not only baptized with water, but with the Holy Spirit.

People: God has given us the same gift that he gave the apostles when we believed in the Lord Jesus Christ.

Pastor: Friends, believe the Good News!

People: In Jesus Christ, we are forgiven.

[AND]

Exhortation

Jesus has given us a new commandment: "Love one another as I have loved you. By this all will know that you are my disciples, if you have love for one another."

PRAYER OF THE DAY

Creator God, you have come to us in this old world in Jesus of Nazareth. Teach us to love without limit, and prepare us for the new heaven and earth where you will again be near enough to us to wipe away the last tear and receive us into the joyful marriage of the church with her Savior, Jesus Christ. Amen

PRAYER OF THANKSGIVING

When we meditate on the glorious splendor of your majesty, O God, we are inspired to proclaim the fame of your abundant goodness. You have marvelously created all things great and small. You care for the sparrow and for the spiral galaxies. Your love is more personal in Jesus Christ, and none of us are forgotten. You will create again a new heaven and a new earth. Your kingdom is an everlasting kingdom, and your gracious rule endures through all generations. We bless your holy name. Amen

PRAYER OF DEDICATION

Sovereign God, with all your works and with all your saints, we give thanks to you and bless your name. Use your church in the power of the Spirit to do more great things for the renewal of your world and all humanity, through Jesus Christ. Amen

PRAYER OF INTERCESSION AND COMMEMORATION

Loving God, you so loved the world that you gave your only Son Jesus for its salvation. You have taught us to pray for all kinds of people in all kinds of circumstances, so hear us as we exercise the priestly role with which you have entrusted us.

Great Physician, remember your suffering children wherever they are. Graciously visit the sick with your healing power. Comfort the old and bedridden and such as are homeless and destitute of friends. Save, O Lord, those who have been driven to despair, the suicidal, the insane. Console those who mourn their dead, especially those who survive the death of a loved one at the hands of the murderous. Sustain us all with faith in your resurrection from the dead as firstfruits of our future with you.

God of all, remember our country and all of us who live here. Safeguard the liberties which our ancestors won by sacrifice and grant to us all a sober and vigilant mind lest through neglect of our neighbors and irreverence toward you we forfeit our freedom.

God, keep in health and safety all who lead our government at every level. Instruct our lawgivers with wise and safe measures. Prosper all who seek to conduct their business with integrity and uphold them under pressure to do otherwise.

Son of God, Son of Mary, King and head of the church, may we envision you in glory in the midst of the seven golden lampstands, clothed with a long robe and with a golden sash across your chest.

Remember your whole church in all its branches. Remove not our lamp out of its place, but tend and replenish the light you have lit in every place. So may your Church more holy live and every lamp more brightly burn.

Wise God, you have created all of us in your likeness. Save us from ignorance, from false images of your being, from the worship of monetary power, and from the deification of religious, entertainment, or sports stars. Send your light and truth to those who still live in the darkness of superstition and fear.

Eternal God, we are grateful for all who have served you in ages past, for all true teachers, reformers, and builders of your holy church. We praise you for all in our own lifetime in whom we have seen your hallowed life, who glorified you in humble faith and have passed into glorious light, leaving us a blessed memory and example. Strengthen us in faith and obedience, that with them who were faithful and patient to overcome, we may be given to eat of the Tree of Life, which grows in the Paradise of God.

All our prayers we offer before your throne, O God, through Jesus Christ our great high priest who ever lives and rules beside you in the communion of the Holy Spirit, one God, time without end. Amen

Sixth Sunday of Easter

First Lesson - Luke records another vision that guides an apostle to a broadening ministry in the larger world. Acts 16:9-15

Psalm 67

Second Lesson - The glory of the New Jerusalem is synonymous with the glory of God. Revelation 21:10, 22–22:5

Gospel - Making ready for his departure, Jesus prepares the disciples to receive the Holy Spirit as their new teacher. John 14:23-29
[OR]
The presence of Jesus and the authority of his directions bring instant healing and strength to an invalid. John 5:1-9

CALL TO WORSHIP

Leader: The grace of our Lord Jesus Christ be with you all.

People: And also with you.

Leader: Be glad and sing for joy,

People: because God judges the peoples with justice and guides every nation on earth.

INVOCATION

Joyfully, we come before you, though to be in your presence strikes us with awe, O God, Creator and Judge of all the worlds. We come only in the confidence of the brothers and sisters of Jesus Christ inspired by his living and loving Spirit. For their sakes receive us; through the same Jesus Christ our Savior. Amen

PRAYER OF CONFESSION

God of law and love, your Son came preaching that the law was made for us and not that we were made for the law. Forgive us if we have made commandments for others to follow where you have not made any. Excuse any zeal that commands what he taught rather than teaches what he commands. Recall us from any thoughtless talk and speculation, without the guidance of the Holy Spirit, that disturbs the faith and peace of mind of others. Prevent us from adding unnecessary burdens to ourselves and others when Jesus calls us to bear an easy yoke and carry a light burden, for his sake. Amen

Declaration of Pardon

Pastor: Friends, hear the Good News! Jesus says: Set your troubled heart at rest, and banish your fears.
People: Peace is Christ's gift to us.
Pastor: Friends, believe the Good News!
People: In Jesus Christ, we are forgiven.

[AND]

Exhortation

Heed the word God speaks through the living Word, Jesus. Heed the word the Spirit teaches, calling to your mind the teaching of Jesus. In this way show your love for God despite those who do not heed what Jesus says.

PRAYER OF THE DAY

Open our eyes, Divine Healer, that we may see glorious visions of what you will accomplish for humanity at the end of time. Open our ears that we may hear, and open our hearts that they may heed the words that you say. Let our love for you be made evident by our readiness both to trust and to obey your guidance by the Holy Spirit. Amen

PRAYER OF THANKSGIVING

We are thankful for glimpses of blue skies through clouds of trouble, good creator, for visions of a beautiful city beyond the dirt and grime, the pollution and crime of our earthly cities. We long for peace amidst the tensions, the conflicts, the terrorism, the open war of our world. We treasure the inner peace that you give us, making our survival possible in times of stress and uncertainty. We dream of the paradise of undisturbed peace, your realm of justice unshakeable, where you rule unopposed, Monarch of peace, Prince of peace, Spirit of peace. Amen

PRAYER OF DEDICATION

O God, you have blessed us with land that bears fruit after blossom time and vines that bear grapes after pruning and tying time. We offer to you our offerings in thanksgiving and our lives to be fruitful in good works that our society may not be barren and without your grace made manifest in us by the Spirit. Amen

PRAYER OF INTERCESSION
AND COMMEMORATION

Spirit of God, pour God's love into our hearts so that we may pray for others as we pray for ourselves. Grant to your church the faith that can move mountains, the trust that the old can be made new, the love   that includes those whom others have abandoned. Continue to send your church to places without a house of prayer, to children without a school, to the sick without a doctor or nurse. Bless those who translate the Bible into languages in which the Good News has not yet been read. Grant to all your people wisdom and courage to share their faith with those who live in doubt or anger and despair.

Supreme Ruler over all, at every level give our leaders prudence and the strength to maintain order and good government. Bless all who work to increase employment and those who serve the unemployed. May we share the prosperity that results from the cooperation of people in business and industry, in government and labor unions.

God for all seasons, you have promised that seedtime and harvest shall not cease and that the earth would be fruitful and multiply with the good things that supply our needs. Bless all who till the soil and sow the fields, dairy farmers and those who raise our meat. Grant seasonable weather for crops and orchards. Give us reason for rejoicing when time for harvesting comes.

Lord Jesus, as of old the sick were brought to you for healing, so in our prayers we bring you the sick in body, mind, and spirit, knowing your love and healing power. Increase their trust in you and the gifts of healing you have given to medical teams of doctors, nurses, and technicians. Bless those gathered in self-help groups to aid in the recovery of those who are addicts and their co-dependents. True freedom is your gift and saving grace freely given.

God of grace and glory, we are grateful for the countless multitude of the dead who died in the Lord, and especially our own dear ones whom you have taken from the conflicts of this life to the peace of the world unseen. Preserve us as we persevere in the faith so that at the last we may share the glory of your immediate Presence. We hallow your name, one God, fatherly, brotherly, motherly. Amen

Seventh Sunday of Easter

First Lesson - The experiences of Paul and Silas in Philippi make one of the most exciting stories of the early church. Acts 16:16-34

Psalm 97

Second Lesson - The last word of the book of Revelation and the last word of the canon is the grace of our Lord Jesus Christ. Revelation 22:12-14, 16-17, 20-21

Gospel - This great prayer of Jesus is for the unity of the whole community of his disciples. John 17:20-26

CALL TO WORSHIP

Leader: The grace of our Lord Jesus Christ be with you all.
People: And also with you.
Leader: Sing praises to God, who is monarch of all the earth;
People: We will sing praises to God with a psalm.

INVOCATION

With psalms and hymns and spiritual songs we come to worship you, O God, confessing our sins and seeking your pardon and our peace. Receive us for the sake of Jesus Christ in whose name with yours and the Holy Spirit we were baptized. Amen

PRAYER OF CONFESSION

Holy God, neither through the doors of this house nor through the gates of your eternal city may we enter worthily without your forgiveness and the washing symbolized in baptism. We need the ministry of the Spirit to create in us the desire for the finest things that life offers. Forgive our passions for lesser things unworthy of the princes and princesses

of your royal house, brothers and sisters of the royal Jesus.
Amen

Declaration of Pardon

Pastor: Friends, hear the Good News! Jesus prays for us
who have believed in him through the word of the
apostles.

**People: Jesus prays that we may be with him where he is
with the Father.**

Pastor: Friends, believe the Good News!

People: In Jesus Christ, we are forgiven.

[AND]

Exhortation

Keep the words of this book. Worship God who is the Alpha
and the Omega, the first and the last, the beginning and the
end. Commit yourself to God in life and in death.

PRAYER OF THE DAY

One God of one people, draw us into such close union with
Jesus and with you that all the world may know that Jesus
was sent by you, to love us in your name as in his own. Fill
us with overflowing love to those now feeling unloved who
may learn that you have a place for them as well through
Jesus our Savior. Amen

PRAYER OF THANKSGIVING

All true majesty is yours, O God. You rule over all nations.
Prince of the people, you gather us around you. Eternal
Spirit, you share the glory of Jesus, the exalted Son, with all
who believe in him through the hearing of the gospel. We
rejoice in the privilege of calling upon your name revealed to
us by Jesus Christ and the church which is his bride. We
celebrate the victories you have won and have yet to win until
the day of his re-appearing. Accomplish the purposes of your

love established before the creation, uniting us as one, as you are one, the Transcendent, the Incarnate, the Universal. Amen

PRAYER OF DEDICATION

Your gift of life is priceless, living One. We cannot repay nor match your generosity, but we can testify to your goodness through the church and personally, for the sake of Jesus Christ. Amen

PRAYER OF INTERCESSION
AND COMMEMORATION

Eternal God, to whom has ascended our Lord Jesus Christ, head of the church in heaven and earth, hear our prayers for the church everywhere in the world, born of the Spirit who proceeds from you both.

May the same Spirit of truth purge the church of all unbelief and superstition, all heresy and factitious opinion. Unify the church in one Lord, one faith, one baptism, bringing us all to one holy Table in celebration of the salvation won for us by our ascended Lord. May the church in its several branches learn to work in more manifest unity to the glory of your name. May all of us as living members of your church work faithfully under the guidance of the Holy Spirit all the days of our lives.

Ruler of all rulers, bless our elected officials, our legislators, and all who exercise authority over us, that they may see you before them always as their ruler and guide. Give to our diplomats the spirit of integrity that they may deal honestly with other nations for the good of the international family of nations. Save the United Nations from corruption and division that the greatest gifts of human culture may be shared generously among all people. Hasten the day when all shall serve you in reverence and all others as brothers and sisters who worship you as in one family.

Holy God, you have been revealed in both mercy and severity. Restrain those tempted to evil. Lift up the fallen, free those enslaved by human oppression or by chemical addiction. Give searchings of conscience to those who blaspheme your name, and save us all from our sins.

Shepherd and Bishop of our souls, comfort all who are lonely and sad, the sick and the suffering, the infirm and the dying. Remember those we can name and those we do not know. As you sent Jesus to be a healer among us, so call good physicians in every generation to use their gifts in the care of the sick and the cure of disease. Bless also all who do research that new medicines and procedures may be found to heal our ailments.

God of all spheres, who has received our Lord Jesus Christ out of our sight and with him in our own time the faithful in the hour of their death, so may we live out our days with implicit trust in your grace that at the last we too may be received into the place being prepared for all who love you.

All our prayers and intercessions we offer in the name above all earthly names, Jesus Christ our Lord, who with you, O God, and the Holy Spirit is worthy to receive all glory and praise, now and forever. Amen

Pentecost

First Lesson - The Spirit of God bridges language barriers to begin the creation of one church for Jesus Christ. Acts 2:1-21 [OR]
The confusion of language can bring to a halt human cooperation and empire building. Genesis 11:1-9

Second Lesson - Paul reminds the Romans that the Christian family spirit is created by the Spirit of God.   Romans 8:14-17 [OR]
Acts 2:1-21

Gospel - Jesus promises that with the coming of the Spirit his disciples will do even greater things than he has done. John 14:8-17 (25-27)

CALL TO WORSHIP

Leader: The grace of our Lord Jesus Christ be with you all.

People: And also with you.

Leader: Sing to the Eternal One as long as you live;

People: we praise our God while we have any breath.

INVOCATION

All-hearing God, we will sing to you as long as we have life and breath, and when there is no longer sufficient breathe to praise you aloud, we will praise you in our hearts and minds. Divine Spirit, inspire our minds and our songs now and every day, and we will praise you; through Jesus Christ our Lord. Amen

PRAYER OF CONFESSION

Universal Spirit, Human Spirit, Eternal Spirit, we confess our fear of the unknown, the strange culture, the unpredictable future, the threat of disease, of misfortune, of war, and of death. The powers of evil in the world are strong, and we are anxious lest they overpower us and take us out of your hands. You have offered us the gifts of peace, the continuing instruction of the Holy Spirit, but we have neglected those things that belong to our peace. Forgive us for the sake of Jesus Christ, crucified, risen, and ascended. Amen

Declaration of Pardon

Pastor: Friends, hear the Good News! The Holy Spirit has been sent to be our helper.

People: The Holy Spirit has been sent to banish our fears and to give us peace.

Pastor: Friends, believe the Good News!
People:**In Jesus Christ, we are forgiven.**

[AND]

Exhortation

Have faith, the day of God's peace will come. Go forward with Christ to meet it.

PRAYER OF THE DAY

Giver of peace, banish our fears and our sense of loneliness. Call to our minds all that Jesus has told us and strengthen us to follow faithfully and to speak clearly of your love for all in Jesus Christ, the Savior of the world. Amen

PRAYER OF THANKSGIVING

Universal Mind, universal Linguist, universal Advocate, we are thankful that you reveal yourself in many thoughts and ideas, in many languages and varieties of music, in many ministries of teaching, worship, hearing, and helping. We rejoice in the work of translators that have made the Old Testament and New Testament speak our language and more than a thousand other languages of the world. We sing your praise in many accents, in many tempos, in many harmonies, knowing that you love variety. How wonderful is the diversity in nature that you have created, God of beauty, truth and love. Amen

PRAYER OF DEDICATION

Eternal Spirit, on this special day we give our offerings freely and gladly in the knowledge that you are at hand. You are praised today around the world, in many different places, in different languages, with multiple gifts. Receive us with our gifts for we are yours, through Jesus Christ our Lord. Amen

PRAYER OF INTERCESSION
AND COMMEMORATION

O God of power with might to shake all the nations, you have sent your Son to be the treasure of all nations, and the Holy Spirit to fill his church with splendor. Grant to your preachers sincere discourse to proclaim your Word not with plausible words of popular wisdom, but with a demonstration of the Spirit and of power so that wayward and careless people may be turned to you, and all your servants be roused to serve you with greater ardor, courage, and fidelity. So re-empower your church that the cause of Christ may prosper in villages and cities across this country and around the world. Will you not revive us again, so that your people may rejoice in you and your name, so commonly taken in vain by many, may again be honored?

Hear us, O God, for the good of the land you gave to our ancestors. Protect our nation from crime and mischief, and let godliness more and more hallow our common life.

Give health and grace to all who make and administer our laws. Bless our industries and teach both labor and management to work honestly and heartily that there may be enough and to spare for everyone. Deliver the needy when they call, the poor and those who have no helper. Teach the rich not to be proud, covetous, and luxurious, but rather to be humble, temperate, and gracious, not trusting in uncertain riches, but so using their earthly possessions in all kinds of good deeds, as not to lose the heavenly treasure. Remember all who are mindful of the lonely and the forgotten and all who in the compassion of Christ serve the needs of the poor.

Surround with your favor the lives of those bound up with ours. Bless our children and grandchildren, and may our family life together be a school of everyday religion.

Comfort the mourning and grant your mercy to the sick who look to us for our prayers. Grant them healing and strength according to their age and to those near death a peaceful release from all suffering.

113

Finally, grant us all, O God, a place and portion with your saints in glory. We give you thanks and   praise for them and their good example to us. May we follow in their footsteps to our home above where the light of your presence shines undimmed. To you, God of pure light, to you, Light of the world, to you, Light of our own hearts, we give all honor and dominion. Amen

After Pentecost

Trinity Sunday

First Lesson - Wisdom is personified similarly as the Word is made personal. Proverbs 8:1-4, 22-31

Psalm 8

Second Lesson - To know God is to grow in spiritual maturity. Romans 5:1-5

Gospel - Jesus promises further extension of the understanding of the things of God. John 16:12-15

CALL TO WORSHIP

Leader: The grace of our Lord Jesus Christ be with you all.

People: And also with you.

Leader: Let us exult in the hope of the divine splendor and even in our present suffering.

People: We know that endurance gives proof that we have stood the test and our hope will not be mocked.

INVOCATION

God-of-eternity, God-in-our-history, God-in-our-today, we come to worship you and to celebrate the names in which we have been baptized: Father, Son, and Holy Spirit. As we hear your Word expand our concept of your mysterious Being that we may pray with deeper reverence in the name of Jesus Christ. Amen

PRAYER OF CONFESSION

God of wisdom, we have difficulty accepting ourselves as we are. We sometimes act as if we knew as much as you do. At other times we put ourselves down as knowing nothing. You have given us a responsible place in the order of your creation, and we sometime abdicate that responsibility for the

116

ecology. You have given us places of responsibility in the church, and we too often push it off on others. Forgive our irresponsibility and false pride, and help us find ourselves in Jesus Christ our Lord. Amen

Declaration of Pardon

Pastor: Friends, hear the Good News! We have been justified through faith in Jesus Christ.

People: We have been received into the sphere of God's grace.

Pastor: Friends, believe the Good News!

People: In Jesus Christ, we are forgiven.

[AND]

Exhortation

Let us continue at peace with God through our Lord Jesus Christ and share with others the love with which the Holy Spirit floods our hearts.

PRAYER OF THE DAY

You have given us the Holy Spirit, Christ Jesus, to enable us to share your peace with others. Prepare us to speak your word of judgment and forgiveness as readily as we receive your judgment and forgiveness ourselves, for your own name's sake. Amen

PRAYER OF THANKSGIVING

Your wisdom, O God, is beyond all understanding, beyond our individual comprehension and beyond all the gathered wisdom of humanity. We are humbled by the glories of the heavens and the earth, by the powers of the wind and the tide and volcanos, by the energies of living things and chemicals, by the complexities of the relationships of all you have created. We are grateful for all the good gifts you have given us and the grace to use them for the benefit of humanity. We

117

are thankful for the guidance you will continue to give us as we seek new ways to recover the balance of nature and full sharing with all your creatures. We glorify you, Initiator, Investor, Integrater, one God, forever. Amen

PRAYER OF DEDICATION

Your greatness is seen, O Lord, our Lord, in all the world. Receive our offerings as a sign of our obedience to your mandate to manage wildlife and garden the earth, to preserve life and enrich all humanity; through Jesus Christ our Lord. Amen

PRAYER OF INTERCESSION
AND COMMEMORATION

God of all life, you have planted your church, a tree of life in the midst of the world. Keep strong your planting, preserving every branch from any blight of unbelief and canker of hypocrisy, from barrenness and withering. Protect it from the blast of mockery and wicked hands that would break it down. Prune your church of deadwood and make it fruitful in all good works and its leaves for the healing of the nations in union with the root and trunk of the tree, Jesus Christ our Lord.

God of all nations, bless the United Nations so that all your people everywhere may live with governments which are accountable to each other and to you. Bless all heads of government that they may seek your wisdom and grace to govern with rectitude. May every judge from the World Court to the local magistrate seek your truth and true justice with mercy.

Dispose workers and tradesmen, merchants and industrialists, bankers and financiers, sport and entertainment personalities, to consider not what the world allows, but what your law commands so that all robbery and ill-gotten gain may be hateful in our sight as in yours. May truth and justice be the stability of our times and our deepest trust be not in any human institution but in the rule of Christ whose dominion shall not pass away.

Father of all mercies, compassionate Son of God, Holy Spirit of God, continue the healing ministry of Jesus among the sick in every generation. Bless every person with healing gifts, every clinic, hospital, and hospice that cares for the sick and dying. Bless all who counsel the mentally disturbed, the addicted, and the confused. Bless pastors and church counselors who seek to help the doubting and the lost to find the truth.

Bless nursing mothers and their babies, young children and those who will, in mind, always be children. Grant to those who are of advanced years a happy and thankful old age and hope of the better life that awaits beyond death.

We bless you for all faithful souls who now live in everlasting peace with you. Direct our life in faith and good works so that our passage through the world may bring us to the place of rest you have prepared for all saints. Unto you, Father, Son, and Holy Spirit, ever-living and holy Trinity in Unity, be all glory and praise time without end. Amen

Proper 4 (May 29 - June 4)

First Lesson - Elijah and the prophets of Baal meet in a dramatic confrontation. 1 Kings 18:20-21 (22-29), 30-39

Psalm 96:1-13

Second Lesson - Paul expresses dismay that the Galatians have so soon turned away from the freedom of the gospel he has preached to them. Galatians 1:1-12

Gospel - Jesus heals the slave of a foreign soldier on duty in Galilee. Luke 7:1-10

CALL TO WORSHIP

Leader: The grace of our Lord Jesus Christ be with you all.

People: And also with you.

Leader: Ascribe to the Lord the glory due his name;

People: We bring an offering and come into his courts.

INVOCATION

God of majesty, Christ of Calvary, Spirit of love, with what mixed feelings we address your throne of justice and mercy. Hear our petitions as they are pleasing to you, and grant us our desires as they are in accordance with your holy will; through Jesus Christ our Lord. Amen

PRAYER OF CONFESSION

Constant God, we confess our inconsistency. We are too often prone to seek favor with people than to risk disapproval of Christian convictions. We are prepared to rationalize or reinterpret difficult demands of Jesus and compromise our relation to him rather than put ourselves at odds with common practice. Forgive our waffling that gives an uncertain impression as to our real commitment, whether it is to the Good News or popular opinion. We do trust in your mercy, through Jesus Christ the Savior. Amen

Declaration of Pardon

Pastor: Friends, hear the Good News! Our Lord Jesus Christ sacrificed himself for our sins to rescue us out of the present age of wickedness.

People: Grace and peace are ours through the mediation of Christ with our Creator.

Pastor: Friends, believe the Good News!

People: In Jesus Christ, we are forgiven.

[AND]

120

Exhortation

Having been called by grace, do not turn away in search of any other gospel. Don't let anyone unsettle your mind with distortions of the Good News of Christ. Be a faithful servant of Jesus.

PRAYER OF THE DAY

Help us to be faithful intercessors, good Lord, ready to pray for others as readily as for ourselves. Let our prayers reflect our humility before you. Save us from taking to ourselves any credit for the good response that you give and the great things that you do, through Jesus Christ. Amen

PRAYER OF THANKSGIVING

God of all peoples and nations, receive the praise directed to you by whatever title or name in whatever language or ritual, by whatever race or nation. You are worthy of the highest praise, the purest thought, the most precious offering of beauty and service. We thank you for the disclosure of yourself made through Jesus Christ, and we are dedicated to share the Good News about him with our neighbors, that others may join in our hymns of thanksgiving to your name. Amen

PRAYER OF DEDICATION

Divine Savior, we cannot buy the salvation you freely give. Our offerings can help spread the Good News, in word and work, in this place and every place as your people fulfill the commission given by the risen Christ. Amen

PRAYER OF INTERCESSION
AND COMMEMORATION

To our thanksgiving and praise, O God, we add our prayers for the church of Jesus Christ that it may have the goodwill of all the people and that day by day you will add to our number those who are being saved. Fulfill the hope of our Lord Jesus that when he is lifted up from the earth, he will draw all people to himself. Bring honor to the name of him who though despised and rejected in the earth was received in resurrected glory in heaven.

Fulfill his promised presence by the Holy Spirit everywhere in the church but especially in remote areas to which the church has gone to make disciples of all nations. Bless both the preaching and the teaching ministry of the church so that those baptized in the name of the Father and of the Son and of the Holy Spirit may learn to obey everything that Jesus has commanded.

Bless all who are called to be our leaders that they may uphold the law, curb lawlessness, and relieve the powerless. Give success to those who seek to uproot networks of crime and illegal drug distribution.

Continue among us an appropriate reverence for human life. May our physicians and nurses, medical technicians and social workers emulate the gentle approach of Jesus the healer. Give them skill of mind and hand that they may both heal the body and relieve the mind. Give them wisdom in consulting both with their patients and with those concerned about their patients.

Comforting Spirit, bring cheer to the discouraged, rest to the weary, health to the sick in body, mind, or spirit. Give to the bereaved the oil of gladness instead of mourning, the mantle of praise instead of a faint spirit. Relieve any fears of the dying with the promise of   eternal life in Christ. We rejoice in the good news that because Jesus has overcome death, we also will live. We are encouraged by the witness of your apostles who saw Jesus alive and ascended to you. Into your keeping we have committed our beloved dead. Like him who was dead but is alive for evermore, so we believe are those whom we see here no longer. Keep us ever in this faith, that we may bear the heat of the day, knowing that there will be at last the rest of eternity in everlasting peace. To the risen

Christ our Savior, to you who raised him from death, and to the Holy Spirit be ascribed all glory and dominion now and forever. Amen

Proper 5 (June 5-11)

First Lesson - The "bottomless barrel" is a sign of God's providence to the widow and the prophet who is her guest. 1 Kings 17:8-16 (17-24)

Psalm 146

Second Lesson - Paul defends the authenticity of his gospel as being truly a revelation of God. Galatians 1:11-24

Gospel - Another resuscitation of a widow's son gives the people a reason to have hope that another prophet like Elijah has come. Luke 7:11-17

CALL TO WORSHIP

Leader: The grace of our Lord Jesus Christ be with you all.

People: And also with you.

Leader: Happy are you whose help is the God and Father of our Lord Jesus Christ.

People: We are happy for our hope is in our God, who keeps faith forever.

INVOCATION

Eternal God, we worship you, for you lift us up when we are bowed down, you love us as if we were as righteous as your Son Jesus. We look to you to execute justice for the oppressed, to give food to the hungry, to set the prisoner free, and to open the eyes of the blind; in the name of Jesus Christ. Amen

PRAYER OF CONFESSION

God of the living, we are more apt to chide you in the untimely death of a member of our families or one of our friends than to mourn what humankind has done to your incarnate Son, Jesus of Nazareth. When you have spared our lives in serious illness or accident, we have vowed in our thanksgiving to serve you without stint, but soon take life for granted again and forget our vows. Forgive us for the sake of him, who, for our sins, was crucified and raised from the dead, even Jesus Christ. Amen

Declaration of Pardon

Pastor: Friends, hear the Good News! The revelation of God's grace in Jesus Christ has been preached to both Jew and Gentile.

People: We have experienced God's favor in Christ our Savior.

Pastor: Friends, believe the Good News!

People: In Jesus Christ, we are forgiven.

[AND]

Exhortation

The Good News you have heard is not for you only, but for everyone. Pass it on.

PRAYER OF THE DAY

Lord of life and conqueror of death, we do not expect you to give us the power to raise the dead, but you can share your compassion with us, so that our hearts go out to the bereaved. Use our presence, by words of hope and gestures of helpfulness, to ease their sorrow, in your name. Amen

PRAYER OF THANKSGIVING

Unchanging God, Man of sorrows and joy, life-giving Spirit, we rejoice that in your favor there is life. Tears may linger at nightfall, but joy comes in the morning. When you turn your face from us we are filled with dismay, but when you smile upon us we are clothed with joy. We strip off the sackcloth of despair and put on baptismal robes of holiness and everlasting life by the grace of our Lord Jesus Christ. Amen

PRAYER OF DEDICATION

Let us give you our life, day by day, as long as we live, timeless God, until in death you take us to higher service. Then perfect us in that service to which we are now apprenticed in Jesus Christ. Amen

PRAYER OF INTERCESSION
AND COMMEMORATION

Mighty God, you have commanded us to make prayers and supplications for all people. Hear our intercessions in the name of Christ.

We pray for our relatives and friends, near or far, for all who love us and pray for us and all who trust us to remember them in prayer. Teach us how to love and pray for strangers and to contribute to their needs and extend hospitality to them. Enable us by the Spirit to befriend strangers to the covenants of promise who have no hope and live without you in the world despite your desire to be their God also.

Comfort the lonely, encourage the depressed, heal the sick, mend the broken, and send help to the powerless. Make us strong to do what we can and humble in knowing what is beyond our power to remedy.

Keep our country true to its highest ideals, and where our actions have fallen short of our ethics grant us the will to change and serve the commonwealth more diligently.

Open to our children and their teachers the treasures of holy wisdom. Illumine their minds with the truth of Christ. With the advance in knowledge and science grant a comparable growth in grace and love of neighbor.

May your church be a continuing example of reformation addressing new issues with new insights that the Spirit will give as we study the Word of God written and seek the guidance of the living and eternal Christ.

Give us patience to live our years of preparation in the school of experience so that we are ready for the commencement of higher learning in the university of heaven and prepared to worship you worthily in that great company; through Jesus Christ our Lord, to whom with you, and the Holy Spirit, be ascribed all wisdom, love, and power. Amen

Proper 6 (June 12-18)

First Lesson - Divine judgment is promised by the prophet Elijah against the greedy and unjust rulers who prey on the weak. 1 Kings 21:1-10 (11-14)

Psalm 5:1-8

Second Lesson - Paul confesses that his justification is through Christ and not the law that was his heritage as a Jew. Galatians 2:15-21

Gospel - In the house of a Pharisee Jesus receives the attention of a sinner and uses the occasion to tell a parable and issue a pardon. Luke 7:36–48:3

CALL TO WORSHIP

Leader: The grace of our Lord Jesus Christ be with you all.

People: And also with you.

Leader: Enter God's house through the abundance of God's steadfast love. Pray humbly in reverence of God's holiness.

People: We pray humbly in reverence of God's holiness. When we leave we will make our way straight before the eyes of God.

126

INVOCATION

Almighty God, holy and just, no earthly monarch can approach your majesty and justice. With reverence we come through the advocacy of your blessed Son, Jesus Christ. Receive the worship we offer in his Spirit for his name's sake. Amen

PRAYER OF CONFESSION

Supreme Monarch, we acknowledge that we are frequently unthinking in our behavior, needing to be checked in our courses by your word in Christ, in writing, and in the witness of your church. Too often we stonewall, unwilling or afraid to confess that we could be mistaken in what we do and say. We forget the forgiveness that you offer in Christ when we are honest in admitting our mistakes, our misjudgment, our misdeeds. Remind us of the increase of love that can come with the increase of forgiveness through Jesus Christ our Lord. Amen

Declaration of Pardon

Pastor: Friends, hear the Good News! We are made right with God through our faith in Jesus Christ,

People: who loved us and gave himself for us, whose death was not in vain.

Pastor: Friends, believe the Good News!

People: In Jesus Christ, we are forgiven.

[AND]

Exhortation

Live by faith in the Son of God. Be crucified with Christ and let his life be lived out in you.

PRAYER OF THE DAY

Merciful Lord, may all of our worship be adoration for your generous forgiveness and not an attempt to achieve what you have already granted freely. Send us out in peace of mind and heart to share your saving word in Jesus Christ our Lord. Amen

PRAYER OF THANKSGIVING

We rejoice, good Lord, that you have cleared our account of indebtedness to God so that we may serve you in the spirit of gratitude. You have been our refuge in times of distress and have enfolded us in unfailing love. You have sent us not only critics to point out our faults but also your Son to be our Savior, not only the law but also the gospel. How great you are: holy, understanding, loving. Alleluia! Amen!

PRAYER OF DEDICATION

Creator of beauty, Lord of life, you accept graciously not only the practical services we offer to you but also the offerings of the heart, the works of art, and the gestures of love. Receive our gifts of vocation and avocation. All we have we owe to you, through Jesus Christ, our love, our Lord. Amen

PRAYER OF INTERCESSION
AND COMMEMORATION

O God, you have taught us how good it is to follow the promptings of your Spirit and how bitter is the grief of failing to know and do what is good. Forgive our failures and renew our resolve to be obedient to your call to serve you in all the activities of our daily life.

You have created the church to be the guardian of the truth that is Jesus Christ and to share it with others. Make us wise in this vocation, ready to hear what others believe to be the truth, and humble in sharing our own insights.

Bless those who are preparing to teach our children and youth in public and private schools at every level. May they find wisdom in the reading of your written Word and love in the worship of you that will be reflected in their concern for the healthy growth of the immature to maturity in responsibility.

Bless all who confer in the cause of peace that sham and posturing may give way to genuine dialogue and agreements be reached that will bring an end to conflict and bloodshed. Be with all who till the soil and reap the harvest. Protect miners, mariners, flyers, and all who work in hazardous occupations to meet our common needs.

Compassionate Christ, heal those who are sick in body or mind, especially those known and dear to us who look to you for healing and help.

Heavenly Father, we rejoice in the company of all who have confessed you on earth and who have had their names inscribed in the book of life in heaven. Grant us like them to live as more than conquerors so we will be clothed like them in white robes, and our names not blotted out of the book of life but recognized by your Son Jesus as one of his brothers or sisters. To you, O God, with our brother Jesus ascended and the Holy Spirit descended, be ascribed unending love and honor. Amen

Proper 7 (June 19-25)

First Lesson - Elijah seeks to hear the voice of God in a variety of sounds in nature. 1 Kings 19:1-4 (5-7), 8-15a

Psalms 42 and 43

Second Lesson - Paul describes the role of law in bringing the baptized to the dignity of the children of God. Galatians 3:23-29

Gospel - The Creator and Healer also has the power to destroy his creation. Luke 8:26-39

CALL TO WORSHIP

Leader: The grace of our Lord Jesus Christ be with you all.

People: And also with you.

Leader: Come to God's dwelling as to a beacon on a holy hill. Let God's light and truth lead you.

People: We come to the altar of God, to offer our joyful praise with heart and voice and instruments of music.

INVOCATION

In a dark world of lies and deceit, O God, we come to your light and your truth. Receive our praise and hear our prayers that we may be guided by your written Word and by the Word alive in the Spirit of Christ. Amen

PRAYER OF CONFESSION

Living God, you hear as well as speak, you feel as well as act. We are sometimes aware of hurting the feelings of our closest friends, but rarely do we consider that our bad behavior breaks your heart. We are too often like thoughtless children whose actions bring disgrace to the whole family. Forgive our indifference to your expectations, but grant us grace to turn from our sins and to live more nearly like your Son, Jesus Christ. Amen

Declaration of Pardon

Pastor: Friends, hear the Good News! Through faith you are all children of God in union with Christ Jesus.

People: Baptized into union with him, we have all put on Christ as a garment.

Pastor: Friends, believe the Good News!

People: In Jesus Christ, we are forgiven.

[AND]

Exhortation

Leave self behind. Day after day, take up your cross and follow Christ. Only in that risk are you ultimately safe.

PRAYER OF THE DAY

Strong Savior, give such trust in your mission that we may be less anxious for our safety and security and willing to risk more in the living out of our discipleship. We want to confirm our lip service to you in day-to-day obedience to your guidance, with more concern for the needs of others than the cost to ourselves. We would shoulder our own cross as you carried yours, Lord Jesus. Amen

PRAYER OF THANKSGIVING

God of Abraham and Sarah, God of Jesus, Mary, and Joseph, God of our ancestors, we rejoice in your patience with us in the slow progress of our social obedience as followers of Christ. In the church of your beloved Jesus Christ, we have removed the distinction between Jew and Greek, both together becoming the spiritual issue of Abraham and Sarah. After long centuries not only has the discrimination between slave and freeman been diminished, but the existence of slavery abolished. We praise you, liberating God. We anticipate with joy the further freedom of male and female as one person in Jesus Christ. We are heirs together of the promise, redeeming God, for we belong to Christ, your only true Child, Jesus of Nazareth. Amen

PRAYER OF DEDICATION

Universal God, we may worship you anywhere. Grant that where we gather today be not only a place of peace and sanctuary, but also a place of risk-taking and self-giving. May our offerings be an honest expression of our priorities and discipleship in the service of Jesus Christ. Amen

PRAYER OF INTERCESSION
AND COMMEMORATION

Mighty and merciful God, grant us the aid of your Holy Spirit that we may pray earnestly for all your people.

Hear our prayers for all who are distressed and afflicted, the physically disadvantaged, the mentally ill, and all who are sick or suffering after an accident. Hear our prayers for any in particular who come to mind. Bless them and those who care for and attend them that they may be restored to health and relieved of pain may rejoice again in the congregation of your worshipers.

Hear our prayers for all nations beginning with our own for we always need your guidance and protection. Give wisdom to our legislators and judges that we may have good laws fairly administered and adjudicated. Direct our industry and trade that we may have full employment and a fair share of the good things of the earth.

Direct all who seek to guide public opinion, who publish the news of the world in print and in the electronic media. Save them from distorting or falsifying the truth, from seeking to make scandal for its own sake, from invading the privacy of citizens or celebrities.

Inspire artists and authors, dramatists and producers, that they may show forth things lovely and of good report without avoiding the evil that is present in the world.

Bless all who proclaim the gospel, giving them strength of character and will that they may not shrink from declaring the whole purpose of God.

Lord of the living, you have kept us among the living but have led many of our family and friends beyond this life to the assembly of the firstborn who are enrolled in heaven, to the judge of all, and to the spirits of the righteous made perfect. Through Jesus, the mediator of the new covenant, bring us at last to your Holy City, and we will join with the great company of those who praise and adore you. Amen

Proper 8 (June 26 - July 2)

First Lesson - Elisha, the successor to Elijah, is demonstrably blessed with some of his predecessor's spirit. 2 Kings 2:1-2, 6-14

Psalm 77:1-2, 11-20

Second Lesson - Christian freedom is not to be an opportunity for self-indulgence but for growth under the guidance of the Spirit. Galatians 5:1, 13-25

Gospel - The call to discipleship can be avoided with a variety of excuses. Luke 9:51-62

CALL TO WORSHIP

Leader: The grace of our Lord Jesus Christ be with you all.
People: And also with you.
Leader: Call to mind the deeds of the Eternal One.
People: We remember the God who works wonders.

INVOCATION

We leave behind our trivial pursuits, O God, to meditate on what you do and have done for us. Receive our worship and lead us in your holy way, through Jesus Christ our Lord. Amen

PRAYER OF CONFESSION

Merciful Sovereign, we are not fit subjects of your rule. You have shown us the ways of love and forgiveness, but we sometimes turn back to ways of pride and hatred. We are more ready to denounce your enemies than to declare the Good News. We delay obedience to your call with excuses of personal privilege. Forgive our refractory discipleship and our outright disobedience, for Jesus' sake. Amen

Declaration of Pardon

Pastor: Friends, hear the Good News! For freedom Christ has set us free.

People: Through the Spirit by faith we wait for the hope of righteousness.

Pastor: Friends, believe the Good News!

People: In Jesus Christ, we are forgiven.

[AND]

Exhortation

Do not use your freedom as an opportunity for selfish advantage, but through love be servants of one another.

PRAYER OF THE DAY

Deliver us, faithful Son, from deliberate delay and the excuses we use to put off positive action when you call us to follow you in service to the high purposes of God's kingdom and completing our Father's business. Amen

PRAYER OF THANKSGIVING

Our hearts are glad, living God: we pray with joy, for you spare our lives despite disease and accident. You are our refuge in fearful times and bring us out of shadow into the place of pleasantness and peace. We are grateful for a goodly heritage and the noble example of the saints who have gone before us. We delight in them and in you. Amen

PRAYER OF DEDICATION

These gifts are meaningless, good Lord, if your name is on our lips but not in our hearts. Let your Spirit complete the good work begun in us that we may worthily bear the name of Christ. Amen

PRAYER OF INTERCESSION
AND COMMEMORATION

O God, Ruler of all, grant that the state of the world may be such that everywhere doors may be open to the truth of your word so that the saving power of your gospel may spread unhindered everywhere.

Take from the world threat of war. Enable nations to live in genuine community. Teach all to direct the power you have given them to the saving and not the destroying of life. Make all to know this is one world, and those in it must be one. Take from the world all religious intolerance. Help all to remember that there are more ways than one to you, and that you have your own secret stairway into every heart.

Take from all lands all enmity between class and class and party and party. Help all to see beyond their individual interests to the common good. Take from the world all enmity and suspicion between nation and nation, between race and race, between color and color. Help us to find a new sense of community which will transcend color and country and in which we all live as one family parented by you. Take from the world all injustice and poverty, and make this a world where poverty shall cease to fester and where none shall prey on another.

Remember in your mercy the poor and the needy, the friendless and the workless, the widow and widower, the fatherless and all who mourn. Remember the sick and the dying and especially all such dear to us. Satisfy their needs, lighten their sorrow, heal their sicknesses, and lift them up, that being comforted and restored they may be thankful. And to you the Parent eternal, and our heavenly brother Jesus Christ, and the Holy Spirit be glory, thanksgiving, and endless praise. Amen

Proper 9 (July 3-9)

First Lesson - A commander of the army discovers that humility is a prerequisite for divine mercy and healing. 2 Kings 5:1-14

Psalm 30

Second Lesson - Paul ends his letter to the Galatians with warnings and his own witness to survival despite suffering. Galatians 6:(1-6), 7-16

Gospel - Seventy disciples are sent in pairs to carry out the mission of Jesus Christ. Luke 10:1-11, 16-20

CALL TO WORSHIP

Leader: The grace of our Lord Jesus Christ be with you all.
People: And also with you.
Leader: Sing praises to the Eternal as God's faithful ones.
People: We give thanks to God's holy name.

INVOCATION

Eternal God, we hallow your name in praise and prayer. You discipline us with strong love but save us with unmeasured grace. Receive our thankful worship through Jesus Christ our Redeemer. Amen

PRAYER OF CONFESSION

God of justice and mercy, we complain about the harvest of our wild oats, and the sentence that is passed against our crimes. More often than not your mercy is greater than we deserve. We may not be as conspicuous as some in our misdeeds, but however subtle we are, we seek your pardon for greed and exploitation of the weak. Our dispositions are often hardhearted, even though you have called us to seek peace. Be open to our prayers for the sake of Jesus Christ our only Savior. Amen

Declaration of Pardon

Pastor: Friends, hear the Good News! You are granted grace, mercy, and peace through our Lord Jesus Christ.

People: Thanks be to God! We are granted grace, mercy, and peace through our Lord Jesus Christ.

Pastor: Friends, believe the Good News!

People: In Jesus Christ, we are forgiven.

[AND]

Exhortation

Wherever you go share the word of peace, saying, "Peace be to this house." The kingdom of God has come near to you. Be sons and daughters of peace.

PRAYER OF THE DAY

Send us, Lord of the harvest, into your fields of humanity to sow the seeds of peace and to seek the harvest of peace. Grant us a gentle spirit even in the midst of violence and the threat of violence. In this make us like yours Son, Jesus Christ. Amen

PRAYER OF THANKSGIVING

Eternal Parent, stronger than any father or mother, gentler than any father or mother, we rejoice in your care for us your children and your encircling love that seeks to draw your quarreling children into an unbroken family. We are thankful for periods of peace and places of tranquility whenever and wherever we find them. We are grateful for peacemakers who seek to relieve tensions and propose compromises, averting violence and encouraging negotiation. We worship the Son of peace, Father of peace, Mother of peace. Amen

PRAYER OF DEDICATION

You receive the poor and humble, merciful God, so we present our offerings mindful that all is yours and you are not restricted by what we give. May your church always be a servant people serving all in need and never devoted to power and wealth. We would serve in the same lowly way as Jesus of Nazareth. Amen

PRAYER OF INTERCESSION
AND COMMEMORATION

Heavenly Parent of an earthly Son of Mary, grant your living Spirit to your church in powerful persuasion to overcome inertia and reticence to do your work in the world. Bless all who call your people to service, not only the work of prayer, but also the work of repairing what is broken and building what is needed, and joining what is separated, and healing what is diseased and ordering what is disordered.

Correct what is amiss in our political systems. Bring the best persons to places of authority that we may be governed by people of integrity and sensibility. Save us from sloganeering that oversimplifies the path to peace and community.

Grant to us the vision of the beautiful and the good that can be renewed through the gift of wise poets and writers, artists and photographers, film makers and mass media specialists. O God, overcome evil with goodness with our obedient support and action; through Jesus Christ our Lord.

Compassionate God, we do not understand why some are sick and some are well. Jesus did not explain to our satisfaction that "There were also many lepers in Israel in the time of the prophet Elisha, and none of them was cleansed except Naaman the Syrian." We cannot deny, however, the need we feel when overcome by disease or accident. We seek the healing Christ for our own health and for the cure of others' disease.

Loving God, your prophet dreams of a time when no more shall there be an infant that lives but a few days, or an old person who does not live out a lifetime; for one who dies at a hundred years will be considered a youth, and one who falls short of a hundred will be considered accursed. We may grasp after the satisfaction of a long life, but even more for the promise that you will show us your salvation. Our chief hope is in Jesus Christ, crucified in young adulthood, but raised from the dead to give us hope of like resurrection and eternal life. We believe that you have already fulfilled your promised salvation to all who have hoped in you and claim that destiny for ourselves in the grace of our Lord Jesus Christ, who lives at your right hand and with you and the Holy Spirit rules heaven and earth, to whom be majesty and glory forever. Amen

Proper 10 (July 10-16)

First Lesson - The prophet sees God judging the uprightness of the nation like a mason with a plumb line in his hand. Amos 7:7-17

Psalm 82

Second Lesson - Paul begins his letter to the Colossian church with great eloquence. Colossians 1:1-14

Gospel - In a parable Jesus uses a foreigner despised by some of his own people as a worthy example of loving one's neighbor as one's self. Luke 10:25-37

CALL TO WORSHIP

Leader: The grace of our Lord Jesus Christ be with you all.
People: And also with you.
Leader: Worship reverently for God is the supreme judge.
**People: God is the supreme judge who is holy and abso-
         lutely just and powerful.**

INVOCATION

God of creation, of power and justice, we worship you in all humility but with great hope through Jesus Christ. You alone are God, worthy of our worship in the unity of the Trinity manifest in Christ and the coming of the Spirit. Receive our prayers in the name of Jesus Christ. Amen

PRAYER OF CONFESSION

God of law, God of grace, God of love, your plumb line condemns the bowing and tottering walls of unjust society. False religion will fail ultimately for you alone are true and to be worshiped in the Spirit of truth. Forgive any practice of ours that values other things or other persons above your worship. Pardon our infractions of your law and in your mercy grant us your Spirit to help us to live uprightly; through Jesus Christ our Lord. Amen

Declaration of Pardon

Pastor: Friends, hear the Good News! God has chosen to reconcile the whole world to God's self.

People: Through the dear Son we have peace with God through the shedding of Christ's blood upon the cross.

Pastor: Friends, believe the Good News!

People: In Jesus Christ, we are forgiven.

[AND]

Exhortation

Love the Lord your God with all your heart, with all your soul, with all your strength, and with all your mind; and your neighbor as yourself. Do that and you will live.

PRAYER OF THE DAY

Lord of heaven and earth, on our way to your heavenly city we want to be helpful to any who need our assistance. Save us from any false preoccupation with piety that would obscure the needs, both physical and spiritual, of our hurting neighbors. Grant us the spirit of the caring Christ. Amen

PRAYER OF THANKSGIVING

Invisible God in the visible Son, Creator Spirit, holding the universe together, we acclaim your preeminence. We rejoice in the resurrection of Jesus as first-born from the dead. He is the head of the church whom we revere in worship and in daily service. We glorify you, O Creator, Sustainer, Reconciler of a fractious world. Amen

PRAYER OF DEDICATION

Use our gifts, gracious God, to bind up the wounded, to anoint the unnoticed with blessing, and to provide the sacraments for the church through Jesus our Savior. Amen

PRAYER OF INTERCESSION
AND COMMEMORATION

Mighty God, you have taught us in our prayers to remember the needs of all people. Hear our intercessions in the name of Jesus Christ and our supplications for the church of your beloved Son.

Head of the church, whose eyes are like a flame of fire, searching all things, remember the church in its faith and works, its progress and failure, its love and its halfheartedness. Deliver us from false doctrine, from hateful neglect, from unwise distractions, firming our resolves to serve you faithfully as long as life lasts. Make your church truly a morning star, heralding a brighter, better day.

Conserve in our national life the great values of our heritage, and reform our society in striving for the high ideals we have espoused but not yet achieved. May your name be hallowed by all.

Bless all branches of our government, that our lawmakers may themselves be law abiding, and our executive and judicial branches equally of good reputation and entirely trustworthy. Tender your care to all who are in sorrow, trouble, weakness or want.

Especially we pray for those who usually worship with us but are absent due to sickness or failing strength. Be present with those who care for the sick and the aged and all who pray for them. Cheer the hearts of those who see death approaching that they may see beyond death our Risen Lord who lovingly awaits us. To you, O God, Creator, Savior, and Restorer, we ascribe all glory and praise. Amen

Proper 11 (July 17-23)

First Lesson - The prophet promises divine judgement against the injustices of the powerful against the poor. Amos 8:1-12

Psalm 52

Second Lesson - Paul declares the centrality of Jesus Christ in the Creator's plan for the cosmos. Colossians 1:15-28

Gospel - An incident in the life of Jesus emphasizes the need for spiritual priorities. Luke 10:38-42

CALL TO WORSHIP

Leader: The grace of our Lord Jesus Christ be with you all.

People: And also with you.

Leader: Hear the proclamation of Christ,

People: In whom the Word of God is fully known.

INVOCATION

Holy God, just and merciful, you desire our penitent worship and our hunger and thirst for what is good. Holy Jesus, you are the goodness we seek for ourselves. Holy Spirit, you are at work in us to make us more like our Lord Jesus Christ. We worship you, one God, in the name of Jesus Christ. Amen

PRAYER OF CONFESSION

Patient God, you still wait for us to sort out our priorities. We are often busy with trivialities, bemused with the incidental, and not attentive to the eternal. Forgive this failure to prepare for ultimate communion with you and yours. Amen

Declaration of Pardon

Pastor: Friends, hear the Good News! God has chosen to make known to you the mystery of the glory of Christ.

People: The Spirit within us enriches our lives.

Pastor: Friends, believe the Good News!

People: In Jesus Christ, we are forgiven.

[AND]

Exhortation

Strive with all your energy to share the insights you have been given for the sake of the church in this and coming generations.

PRAYER OF THE DAY

Capture our attention, great Teacher, that the truth you tell and the truth that you are, will be our eternal treasure never to be taken from us. Amen

PRAYER OF THANKSGIVING

God of surprises, we are thankful for the casual encounters in which we find you present, the shared meal and the

143

experience of hospitality, the stories by which we come to know each other and you, the books and letters which bridge the span of centuries and the distances of our present world, the media which bring us good news as well as bad and sad. We celebrate your presence wherever and with whomever we are in the communion of the Holy Spirit and all saints through Jesus Christ. Amen

PRAYER OF DEDICATION

Let these offerings and all our gifts for strangers be made in the awareness that you are here as well as in the place of need, the hospital, the prison, the lonely room, that our giving may be more fully appropriate, given reverently and in love. Amen

PRAYER OF INTERCESSION AND COMMEMORATION

Mighty God, Ruler of all, direct those who make and administer and judge our laws and all others in authority over us that, led by your wisdom, they may lead us in the way of righteousness, through our Lord Jesus Christ.

Divine Parent, bless all known to us or unknown that have done us good; those who have helped us by their patience and good advice, by kindnesses great or small, and by their prayers for us. If there are any whom we judge to have wronged us, remove all bitterness from our hearts and theirs that we may be reconciled as your children.

Guard the innocent beset by temptation. Encourage those who are in danger of losing their faith and giving up the good fight. Have mercy on habitual criminals and those who are victims of addiction of one kind or another.

Comfort those who are injured by the carelessness or malice of others; the misunderstood, the misjudged, the defamed, and all who are unjustly used and held down by the inhumane.

144

Be near, O Lord, to the sick and the sorrowing. Uphold all who are trying to bear pain and loss bravely, all who must watch their loved ones suffer, and those whose suffering is unrelieved by the knowledge of your caring. Help them as they have need and restore them through the mercy and power of Christ our Savior.

Eternal God, we bless you for all who, holy and humble of heart, served you here until you received them into heavenly service. Guide and defend us in our earthly service that we may be worthy with them to see you face to face in Jesus Christ our risen Lord and ascended Savior, to whom with you, O God, and the Holy Spirit, be given endless praise and honor. Amen

Proper 12 (July 24-30)

First Lesson - The living parable of the forgiveness of adulterous behavior is used by the prophet at God's direction. Hosea 1:2-10

Psalm 85

Second Lesson - Paul urges continued growth in the faith despite the opposition of those promoting a confining religious legalism. Colossians 2:6-15 (16-19)

Gospel - Jesus teaches persistence in prayer. Luke 11:1-13

CALL TO WORSHIP

Leader: The grace of our Lord Jesus Christ be with you all.
People: And also with you.
Leader: Human as we are, let us intercede with God
People: for ourselves and for our sinful world.

INVOCATION

Transcendent God, approachable God, loving God, we come to worship you in humility and admitting our need of the aid of your Spirit to pray appropriately and in accordance with your will. Receive us as we offer our prayers, our songs, our offerings, and ourselves through Jesus Christ our Lord. Amen

PRAYER OF CONFESSION

Listening God, prayer-teacher, prayer-prompter, we are often perfunctory in our prayers, casual, without expectation of response. We separate our petitions for forgiveness from the need to forgive others; we prevent the discipline that would change us and turn us outward again with persistent concern for others and ongoing intercession for the whole world, not just our own little circle. Hear our request for forgiveness. Give us a forgiving spirit. Lord, teach us to pray. Amen

Declaration of Pardon

Pastor: Friends, hear the Good News! God has forgiven us all our sins,

People: canceling the bond which pledges us to the decrees of the law, nailing it to the cross.

Pastor: Friends, believe the Good News!

People: In Jesus Christ, we are forgiven.

[AND]

Exhortation

Live your lives in union with Jesus Christ, your Lord. Be consolidated in the faith you were taught, and let your hearts overflow with thankfulness.

PRAYER OF THE DAY

Divine Giver, you give us what is good for us. You have given us Christ and the Holy Spirit. We want to be more responsive to those gifts, with prayerful concern for others. Amen

PRAYER OF THANKSGIVING

Infinite God, God embodied in Christ, God embodied in the church, we worship you with deep reverence. We are mystified by your invisibility and by your infinity. We believe without really understanding that your full nature could be embodied in Jesus of Nazareth, fully human, fully divine. We wonder about the new resurrection life you offer us in our baptism that makes us alive with Christ and members of his body, the church. We are grateful for the costly victory of Christ over evil powers on the cross and rejoice in the freedom won for us. Our hearts overflow with thankfulness.

PRAYER OF DEDICATION

Supreme Sovereign, as high as you are, you care for the lowly. Receive our humble offerings and enable us to participate with you in your unfinished work in the world; through Christ our Redeemer. Amen

PRAYER OF INTERCESSION
AND COMMEMORATION

O God, the Parent and Savior of all, we pray for our neighbors as for ourselves, and especially for those who with us call upon you in the name of Jesus Christ. May we go forth from our hour of prayer to add to our faith good works in a godly and happy life with strong hope and unselfish love.

O Lord, safeguard the freedom of us all in this land of liberty under just laws and honest government. Give us leaders who are prayerful and careful. Preserve and perfect good customs. Strengthen wholesome family life and encourage pure and genuine religion.

As your inspiration alone gives us wisdom and understanding inspire our writers and scholars, artists and inventors, researchers and explorers, that all may seek to contribute to our common knowledge and welfare.

We commend to your fatherly/motherly gentleness all who are sick or depressed, especially any who look to us for our prayers. Comfort and relieve them according to their need. Give them patience until their time of trouble and suffering is ended.

To you, Jesus Christ, faithful witness, firstborn of the dead, and ruler of the kings of the earth, who made us to be a kingdom, priests serving God and your Father, to you with the Holy Spirit be glory and dominion forever and ever. Amen

Proper 13 (July 31 - August 6)

First Lesson - The prophet bemoans the infidelity of Israel. Hosea 11:1-11

Psalm 107:1-9, 43

Second Lesson - Paul speaks of moral and spiritual resurrection. Colossians 3:1-11

Gospel - Jesus warns against misplaced values. Luke 12:13-21

CALL TO WORSHIP

Leader: The grace of our Lord Jesus Christ be with you all.
People: And also with you.
Leader: O give thanks to the Lord, for he is good;
People: for his steadfast love endures forever.

INVOCATION

Infinite God, not only did you create us in your likeness but in Christ have become our kin to ransom from the bondage of sin and death. Receive the praise we bring as those you have set free to serve you and our neighbors as ourselves. Amen

PRAYER OF CONFESSION

God above all, you may fairly judge us for living below the level of our potential. Forgive us for being only partly freed from our old natures and our sins when you have made it possible for us to be renewed in the image of yourself, the likeness in which humanity was created and which has been manifest a second time in Christ. The life we have lived is not the full resurrection-life Christ has offered us. Be patient with our slowness in putting on our new nature in Christ Jesus. Amen

Declaration of Pardon

Pastor: Friends, hear the Good News! Potentially, you have died with Christ to sin, and your life is hidden with Christ in God.

People: When Christ who is our life is manifested, then we too will be manifested with him in glory.

Pastor: Friends, believe the Good News!

People: In Jesus Christ, we are forgiven.

[AND]

Exhortation

Discard the old nature with its deeds. Put on the new nature which is constantly renewed in the image of our Maker.

PRAYER OF THE DAY

Save us, merciful God, from self-destruction, from the accumulation of things for our own enjoyment only and not for the enjoyment and benefit of others. Give us the long view, the eternal perspective, that measures richness in divine and social dimensions and prepares us for the shared life of heaven in Jesus Christ. Amen

PRAYER OF THANKSGIVING

God of hope, thank you for the glimpses of glory that lift us out of despair, for the throb of life that heals the disease of the spirit, for the new virtues that displace the old vices. We remember with gratitude the resurrection of Jesus as a sign of spiritual recovery from sin and death to eternal life. We rejoice in the new sterling of that spiritual life in us. Praise is due to you, living God, living Savior, living Spirit, for you conquer death. Amen

PRAYER OF DEDICATION

Creator of all life, Source of all goodness, transform these tangibles into the intangibles of the Spirit that make the church strong to do your work and accomplish your will in the Spirit of Jesus Christ. Amen

PRAYER OF INTERCESSION
AND COMMEMORATION

O God, you have taught us how good it is to follow the promptings of your Spirit and how bitter is the grief of failing to know and do what is good. Forgive our failures and renew our resolve to be obedient to your call to serve you in all the activities of our daily life.

You have created the church to be the guardian of the truth that is Jesus Christ and to share it with others. Make us wise in this vocation, ready to hear what others believe to be the truth, and humble in sharing our own insights.

Hear our prayers for all who are appointed among us to keep the peace and preserve good order. Give them fairness in judgment and patience under provocation.

Bless those who are preparing to teach our children and youth in public and private schools at every level. May they find wisdom in the reading of your written Word and love in the worship of you that will be reflected in their concern for the healthy growth of the immature to maturity in responsibility.

Bless all who confer in the cause of peace, that sham and posturing may give way to genuine dialogue and agreements be reached that will bring an end to conflict and bloodshed.

Be with all who till the soil and reap the harvest. Protect miners, mariners, flyers, and all who work in hazardous occupations to meet our common needs.

Compassionate Christ, heal those who are sick in body or mind, especially those known and dear to us who look to you for healing and help.

God of life and resurrection, we rejoice in the vision of John who looked, and there was a great multitude that no one could count, from every nation, from all tribes and peoples and languages, standing before your throne and before the Lamb, robed in white, with palm branches in their hands. By the grace of our Lord Jesus Christ bring us to join that joyful company who celebrate your mercy: "Salvation belongs to our God who is seated on the throne, and to the Lamb!" Amen and Amen

Proper 14 (August 7 - 13)

First Lesson - The prophet decries the hypocrisy of ritual worship without moral reform and responsibility for the poor. Isaiah 1:1, 10-20

Psalm 50:1-8, 22-23

Second Lesson - A definition of faith precedes an honor roll of the faithful. Hebrews 11:1-3, 8-16

Gospel - Jesus admonishes the faithful to be ready for the unexpected return of their Lord. Luke 12:32-40

CALL TO WORSHIP

Leader: The grace of our Lord Jesus Christ be with you all.

People: And also with you.

Leader: Gather to God, you faithful ones.

People: We have a new covenant with God by the sacrifice of Christ on the cross!

IN VOCATION

Faithful God, receive us also for the sake of Jesus Christ who has offered himself for the sins of the world. Grant us the aid of your Holy Spirit that our worship may be true and without blemish before you. Amen

PRAYER OF CONFESSION

Forbearing God, despite your call for absolute obedience and the rejection of all other gods, we continue to follow old customs and unexamined behaviors. Forgive such disloyal behavior that taxes your patience. Give us opportunity to mend our ways as we become aware of our need to repent and follow Jesus more nearly. We ask this in his name. Amen

Declaration of Pardon

Pastor: Friends, hear the Good News! It is by faith that we win God's approval.

People: We may trust God to keep the promise in Christ.

Pastor: Friends, believe the Good News!

People: In Jesus Christ, we are forgiven.

[AND]

Exhortation

Be ready, because the Son of Man will come at an hour when you are not expecting him.

PRAYER OF THE DAY

Keep us alert, good Spirit, dressed for action and looking for the coming of the Son of Man. We will serve you actively in the days of your absence and with greater joy when we are fully aware of your presence with us. Amen

PRAYER OF THANKSGIVING

Jesus, Master, we rejoice in the appreciation you show for the simplest services we render. You have set us a perfect example of selfless service. We honor as well those like Abraham and Sarah who have followed your leading without knowing your destiny for them. We would give thanks by our daily work as well as by our Sunday liturgy. Praise to you, God of Sarah and Abraham. Praise to you, Son of Mary, Son of God. Praise to you, Spirit eternal, without beginning, without end. Amen

PRAYER OF DEDICATION

Lord of the church, we bring our offerings Sunday by Sunday to keep the work of the church going steadily on, lest you come and find us not at our work and not prepared for your return. Amen

PRAYER OF INTERCESSION
AND COMMEMORATION

God of the universe, hear us as we pray for all humanity, but especially for your church universal, that the goodwill you have toward all may be heard as really Good News. May your Spirit flourish in every branch of the vine which is the living Christ in the world bringing forth fruit in good living and the good wine of sacrificial giving.

Gracious Savior, may your love work an end to divisiveness in the church at every level. Show us how to help rather than hinder, to be constructive rather than destructive, open rather than shut, inclusive rather than exclusive. Let the church be an example of love overcoming strife.

God of our ancestors, bless this land, its leaders, legislators, and judges. Grant that without fear or favor they may maintain the rights of all, tempering justice with mercy and defending those who cannot plead their own cause. Divine Creator and Re-Creator, cleanse the bloodstream of nations that are poisoned by corruption in high and low places. Strengthen forces of law enforcement in pursuit of extensive organizations of crime.

Jesus, friend of sinners, give courage to whose who are subject to severe temptation, and strengthen them against all evil. Man of Sorrows, comfort the bereaved and lonely. Heal the sick and suffering especially those we name before you in the silence of our hearts. According to your will, give renewed health in body and spirit, that your purposes may be fulfilled in the community of your people.

God our Savior, keep us spiritually fit and lively so that we may not become sluggish, but imitators of those who through faith and patience inherit the promises. We have this hope, sure and steadfast, that enters the inner shrine of heaven where Jesus, a forerunner on our behalf, has entered, having become our high priest forever. To our Advocate and Savior, our Creator and Judge, to the Spirit sanctifying us in the church, be ascribed honor and glory now and forever. Amen

Proper 15 (August 14 - 20)

First Lesson - The prophet speaks of Israel in the parable of the vineyard. Isaiah 5:1-7

Psalm 80:1-2, 8-19

Second Lesson - Heroes of the ancient faith are listed by name or by their destiny to complete the honor roll begun in the previous lesson. Hebrews 11:29–12:2

Gospel - Jesus speaks of the divisions that the call to discipleship may bring. Luke 12:49-56

CALL TO WORSHIP

Leader: The grace of our Lord Jesus Christ be with you all.

People: And also with you.

Leader: Fix your eyes on Jesus on whom faith depends from start to finish.

People: That will help us not to lose heart and grow faint.

INVOCATION

We turn, gracious God, from all that would distract us to see you in the face of Jesus Christ. Divine Spirit, clear our sight that our view may not be distorted but worshiping in spirit and truth may perpetuate life eternal; through Jesus Christ our Lord. Amen

PRAYER OF CONFESSION

Steadfast God, we admit that we are easily swayed by the company we are in and their opinions. We find it difficult to speak our deeper convictions in the face of those who disagree and deride our views. We would rather be in the company of those who agree with us and need to find the courage of our convictions. Forgive our fickleness in preferring to tell people what they want to hear. Hear our prayer for the sake of your bold and truthful Son, Jesus Christ. Amen

Declaration of Pardon

Pastor: Friends, hear the Good News! For the sake of the joy that lay ahead of him, Jesus endured the cross, making light of its disgrace.

People: Christ has taken his seat at the right hand of the throne of God, where he intercedes for us.
Pastor: Friends, believe the Good News!
People: In Jesus Christ, we are forgiven.

[AND]

Exhortation

We must throw off every encumbrance, every clinging sin, and run with resolution the race for which we are entered, our eyes fixed on Jesus, on whom faith depends from start to finish.

PRAYER OF THE DAY

When we find ourselves separated from family and friends on issues of principle and obedience to your Word, grant, God of grace, either that we may be found on your side, or that we may possess the humility to discover our error and to cross over to your company with Jesus Christ. Amen

PRAYER OF THANKSGIVING

Perfect Parent, we are grateful for the love which disciplines us, that you are not indifferent to the way we live, that you want us to learn our lessons, to improve our behavior, to share your holiness. We are thankful for the human parents, pastors, teachers, elders, and friends, who have been speaking your Word to us and have been useful to you in the process of our discipline. We value the peaceful harvest of an honest life. All praise to you, spiritual Parent, exemplary Son, Holy Spirit. Amen

PRAYER OF DEDICATION

Use your church, bold Jesus, to seek justice for the weak and the orphan, to see that right is done for the destitute and downtrodden, to rescue them from the power of those who are evil, and to witness to all the world that you rule the nations. Amen

PRAYER OF INTERCESSION
AND COMMEMORATION

Save the innocent, O Lord, from the violence of people hungry for power, whether forces of governments at war with their enemies or anarchists willing to exploit conflict to destroy all lawful authority. Teach people and parties how to reform governments and institutions without destruction or violence or the threat of violence. Deliver us from envy and hatred, from suspicion and craftiness, and from every cruelty which human beings have inflicted on each other. Teach all movements and all nations how greatly we need a Prince of Peace to rule over us all.

Savior, keep in your mercy all those whom we love, our children, our relatives, our friends and acquaintances. Stretch out to them the strong hand of your help in their time of trouble or crisis of decision. Help us faithfully to visit or write to those who are sick or recovering from illness. Use us to bring a word or gesture of comfort to the bereaved. With the light of hope brighten the days of those whose days on earth are numbered. Save us all from despair when the darkness of evil seems to shadow the sun, through your eternal Son, the true light, who shines in the heart of every human being.

God of the living, we give thanks for your great mercy and salvation, and for the blessed dead who have died in the Lord. We rejoice that they rest from their labors and that their deeds follow them. Make us prolific in good deeds also that we may produce more than wood, hay, and straw to be burnt in the refiner's fire, but trusting in our founder Jesus Christ, build on his foundation with gold, silver, precious stones, durable deeds of the Spirit. All glory be yours, O God. Amen

Proper 16 (August 21 - 27)

First Lesson - The book of the prophet Jeremiah begins with an account of his call to the prophetic office despite feelings of inadequacy. Jeremiah 1:4-10

Psalm 71:1-6

Second Lesson - The gospel of Jesus Christ has brought a new approach to God, but reverence is still appropriate. Hebrews 12:18-29

Gospel - Jesus flies in the face of tradition to perform a miraculous healing on the Sabbath. Luke 13:10-17

CALL TO WORSHIP

Leader: The grace of our Lord Jesus Christ be with you all.

People: And also with you.

Leader: Come, everyone. Rejoice at all the wonderful things that Jesus Christ has done and is doing still.

People: We will give thanks and offer to God an acceptable worship with reverence and awe.

INVOCATION

We come to you, O God, on this day of rest and celebration in thanksgiving for the day of our Savior's rising from the grave and in anticipation of the works of salvation he is yet to do. Receive our worship as the Spirit enables us to pray in humble fashion. Amen

PRAYER OF CONFESSION

Holy God, there are times when we would rather not call you Parent because we would prefer to live the undisciplined life. We would rather go our own way and avoid the training you insist on giving us. We like to be easy-going, slack in our morals, haphazard in our prayers, spiritually out of condition. Forgive such denial of our responsibilities as your children, so unlike your true and perfect Son, Jesus Christ, in whose name we pray. Amen

Declaration of Pardon

Pastor: Friends, hear the Good News! By the grace of our Lord Jesus Christ we are called to the assembly of the firstborn who are enrolled in heaven.

People: We are called to God, the judge of all, and to the spirits of the righteous made perfect, and to Jesus, the mediator of a new covenant.

Pastor: Friends, believe the Good News!

People: In Jesus Christ, we are forgiven.

[AND]

Exhortation

Learn from Jesus that the needs of people are more important than rules.

PRAYER OF THE DAY

Teach us your flexibility and compassion, loving Jesus, that we may never avoid serving the needs of the sick because of some rule of propriety or anxiety about criticism from others. Amen

PRAYER OF THANKSGIVING

Generous and gracious God, you have given Israel a rich heritage of faith in the tradition of Abraham, Isaac, and Jacob, the footsteps of Sarah, Rebekah, and Rachel. You have given Christians an honorable name in Jesus Christ. We are happy in the promise that there will be a new heaven and a new earth, in which we shall see your glory and worship you with people of all nations. All praise be given to you, for your constancy is everlasting. Praise to our Parent, stern but for-

159

giving. Praise to your Son, older and wiser. Praise to your Spirit, who makes us brothers and sisters. Amen

PRAYER OF DEDICATION

As you, Holy One, received the offerings of Israel and chose some of them as priests to serve in your temple, accept our offerings as well and designate some of us to serve you in the ordained ministry so that more people and nations shall worship you. Amen

PRAYER OF INTERCESSION AND COMMEMORATION

Almighty God, you have promised to hear our prayers for others in the Name of your Son, Jesus Christ. We pray that you will bless and extend your church. Lead your people from truth to truth, and in the truth from strength to strength.

Bless all those who give themselves to advance your work, all who give of their leisure to train the young in the ways that are right, and all who have left home and family to spread the gospel.

Hear our prayers for our country. Help us to discover and develop further checks and balances in our economic system that will encourage the best effort of every citizen of whatever capability by providing opportunities for work and leisure that are wholesome and fulfilling.

Restrain unjust and presumptuous claims of nation against nation, class against class, ideology against ideology. Grant us the honesty that acknowledges our own fault before pointing out the faults of others. In the midst of conflict and confusion we become impatient for the coming of your perfect kingdom of goodness, peace, and joy. Hear the prayers of those who would be free from the bondage of evil. Give a new vision of goodness to those who have lost sight of it. You are the spring of hope for all who pass through the valley of sorrow and pain. Refresh all who are in despair through anguish of mind or body. Comfort the troubled, heal the sick, turn grief to joy through Jesus Christ our only Savior.

Eternal God, we do not need fortune tellers or astrologers to tell us what is to come hereafter. The life, death, resurrection, and ascension of your Son, Jesus, is enough for us to know that you are God and offer us eternal life as we follow him, who is the Way, the Truth, and the Life. We ascribe to you all power and love and wisdom. Amen

Proper 17 (August 28 - September 3)

First Lesson - The prophet scolds the people for making two sinful choices. Jeremiah 2:4-13

Psalm 81:1, 10-16

Second Lesson - The letter to the Hebrews ends with miscellaneous moral and spiritual admonitions. Hebrews 13:1-8, 15-16

Gospel - Jesus teaches that humility is better than humiliation. Luke 14:1, 7-14

CALL TO WORSHIP

Leader: The grace of our Lord Jesus Christ be with you all.

People: And also with you.

Leader: Sing the praises of God; raise a psalm to the hallowed name.

People: We will be joyful, and exult before the Parent of the parentless, the Companion of the lonely, the One who makes a home for us all.

INVOCATION

No earthly parent supersedes you, O God. No brother or sister loves us as much as our heavenly brother, Jesus Christ.

No human family spirit is as holy and strong as your church. We worship you, O God, Father, Son, and Holy Spirit. Amen

PRAYER OF CONFESSION

Honest God, it is sometimes easier for us to be devious than straightforward, to sidestep the truth than to confront it. We may not tell an outright lie but may avoid disclosing the whole truth. When we are discovered as not completely trustworthy, our relationships become more cautious and uncomfortable. Forgive any pretense at being what we have not yet become. We want to have the reputation of being both fair and generous before we have fully achieved these virtues. Forgive such hypocrisy, and help us to be more like your truthful and true Son, Jesus Christ. Amen

Declaration of Pardon

Pastor: Friends, hear the Good News! Jesus is mediator of the new covenant.

People: His sprinkled blood will purify us and make us worthy of the company of the spirits of good people made perfect.

Pastor: Friends, believe the Good News!

People: In Jesus Christ, we are forgiven.

[AND]

Exhortation

As you have taken the place of humility in the confession of your sins, accept the invitation to the place of honor as one of God's children and citizens of the heavenly city.

PRAYER OF THE DAY

God above all, help us to receive such honors as come to us with modesty, and to be sincere in honoring the achievements of others in the Spirit of your Son, Jesus Christ. Amen

PRAYER OF THANKSGIVING

God of strength and compassion, we rejoice in the downfall of the wicked and the humiliation of the haughty. We exult in the raising up of the fallen and the release of the prisoner. We are filled with gratitude as we remember the many good things you have given us to enjoy in a fruitful land and for the opportunity of sharing our plenty with others. You are patient and kind to prepares us to live together in peace in the heavenly city; through Jesus Christ our Lord. Amen

PRAYER OF DEDICATION

Loving God, increase in us the kindliness that is blessed in the experience of sharing. Use our gifts to start the young on the right road so that even in old age they will not leave it. Use us also to call to your way those who have not yet found it or have wandered from it; through one who is the way, the truth, and the life, Jesus Christ. Amen

PRAYER OF INTERCESSION
AND COMMEMORATION

We pray, O God, for the great family of your church, called and named in Christ Jesus. May all your children, confessing one Parent in heaven, make it evident that they are brothers and sisters of Jesus, by thoughtfulness and love for one another.

We pray for all ministers and missionaries of the gospel, national and international, especially any who are overburdened, tired, and lonely. Grant to them help, rest, and both human and divine companionship. We pray for our fellow Christians who live under the persecution of regimes hostile to the church. Sustain them in faith with courage and hope that in life or in death they may glorify your name.

Bless our land. Increase among us the desire to serve your good purposes. Spread among us a sturdy faith, social purity without false shame, justice without inclemency, firmness without arrogance.

Bless our elected leaders and judges that they may be a strong defense for the wronged, however poor or voiceless, and a restraint of evildoers, however many and powerful. Let goodness and truth be the pillars of the state.

We pray, O God, for the sick and suffering in our homes and hospitals and all such known and dear to us. Save them from depression. Teach them to hope in your word and wait quietly for your healing and help. Cheer them through the word of Christ and raise them from their beds of sickness, and out of all their sorrows, that they and we may rejoice in giving thanks to you; through Jesus Christ our Lord.

In life and in death, O God, you are our keeper. You keep our going out and our coming in from this time on and forevermore. You keep our beloved dead from all evil; and will keep us also in this life and the next. Hallowed be your name. Amen

Proper 18 (September 4 - 10)

First Lesson - The prophet declares the Creator's privilege of breaking and remaking a flawed nation. Jeremiah 18:1-11

Psalm 139:1-6, 13-18

Second Lesson - Paul suggests that a slave may be freed by brotherhood. Philemon 1:1-21

Gospel - Jesus defines the absolute, bottom-line cost of discipleship. Luke 14:25-33

CALL TO WORSHIP

Leader: The grace of our Lord Jesus Christ be with you all.
People: And also with you.
Leader: Come and speak to our gracious Monarch,

People: **God listens to the prayers of the lowly and will give us courage.**

INVOCATION

Sovereign of sovereigns, we come to you confident of being received because your royal Son, Jesus, lived among us as a commoner. Your Spirit urges us to pray and teaches us how we must change to become your royal children. Accept our praise and our petitions in the name of Jesus Christ. Amen

PRAYER OF CONFESSION

Supreme Being from whom our being comes, only God to whom our prayers should be raised, hear our confession. We find it easier to go along with Jesus when there is a crowd. We are not always ready to part company with family and friends when our call is to costly discipleship. We may begin bravely and lose our nerve, forgetting that you can give us courage in the face of challenge and perseverance in the time of fatigue. Forgive us if we have turned back from your Son, not for the disgrace we bring on ourselves, but for the shame we bring to his name. We have no claim but his gracious intercession for us. Amen

Declaration of Pardon

Pastor: Friends, hear the Good News! God gives us grace and peace through Jesus Christ.

People: **Such knowledge is too wonderful for me!**

Pastor: Friends, believe the Good News!

People: **In Jesus Christ, we are forgiven.**

[AND]

Exhortation

Carry your own cross and be a faithful follower of Jesus. Give up anything that prevents your being a loyal Christian.

PRAYER OF THE DAY

Strong One, without your aid there is no way we can confront the forces of evil within us and around us. Without your enablement, there is no way we can begin, continue, and complete the work you want us to do. Discipline our spirits and keep us in the way of a disciple. Amen

PRAYER OF THANKSGIVING

All-knowing God, your wisdom is beyond our reach. We are thankful that you have accommodated yourself to our limited capacity in the sending of your Son into the world. We are glad for the knowledge of you that we have through Jesus of Nazareth, his life, his teaching, his healing ministry. We appreciate the patience of the Spirit who continues to teach us as we are willing to be taught, through experience and the shared wisdom of others in talking, in reading, in listening to radio and television and recordings. We are in awe of you, for what we know, for what we cannot know, for what we have yet to learn. You are the One who is, who was, and who is to come, Almighty and all wise. Amen

PRAYER OF DEDICATION

Sovereign God, you are a compassionate monarch. You hear the cries of the oppressed and have always helped the needy. You take notice of trouble and suffering and are always ready to help. Use us to do your works of mercy in the name of Jesus Christ. Amen

PRAYER OF INTERCESSION
AND COMMEMORATION

God of diversity, teach us tolerance and adaptability that we may live comfortably with the disabled, the exceptional, the brilliant, the dull, the bored, the violent, and all who are misplaced, misunderstood, and misinterpreted. Give help to those who are charged with finding ways for us to live together in community. We give thanks for tests that show us personality problems, questionnaires that tell us of our talents, tasks that exercise our abilities, tools that help us work, counselors who understand us, teachers who guide and direct us, and ministers who teach and forgive us in your name.

Let your love, O Christ, surround the sick, the troubled, the bereaved, the lonely, the misunderstood, the abandoned. May your love also be embodied in the presence of your people who express concern and do what they can to bring medical attention, psychotherapy, social work, flowers, and favors to the sick and the anxious.

Into your hands we commend, O God, the spirits of the dying. We treasure the vision of John that your heavenly palace is not only radiant with your glory, but home-like in your gentle care of those with tears to be wiped from their faces. Bring us at last beyond earth's sorrows to your everlasting joy and peace, through Jesus Christ our Savior, to whom with you and the Holy Spirit be all glory and dominion for ever and ever. Amen

Proper 19 (September 11-17)

First Lesson - The prophet scolds the nation like naughty children. Jeremiah 4:11-12, 22-28

Psalm 14

Second Lesson - Paul describes the grace of God that converted him from a persecutor to a proclaimer of the Good News of Jesus Christ. 1 Timothy 1:12-17

Gospel - Jesus tells the first of a trilogy of parables that express joy at the recovery of the lost. Luke 15:1-10

CALL TO WORSHIP

Leader: The grace of our Lord Jesus Christ be with you all.

People: And also with you.

Leader: Bring to the Sovereign of the ages, immortal, invisible, the only God, honor and glory.

People: We bring to God a humble spirit, for God will not reject a humble and repentant heart.

INVOCATION

In humility and penitence we bow before you, O God, to bring honor to you, turning from behavior that is shameful in your sight. Remember our human frailty and receive our imperfect worship for the sake of your worshipful Son, Jesus Christ. Amen

PRAYER OF CONFESSION

Creator God, you have every right to destroy what you have made. We have disappointed you with the decisions we have made to worship things of less value even than ourselves, much less than you. We have mistaken symbols for reality and have neglected the contemplation of the infinite for the manipulation of the finite, thinking ourselves powerful. Whether by flood or fire, earthquake or storm, cosmic accident or human destruction, you could wipe us off the face of the earth. You are more patient than we deserve and relent from the threat of destruction with which you warn us in anger for our sins. Forgive us and give us time to overcome our stubbornness and intractability, through Jesus Christ our Savior. Amen

Declaration of Pardon

Pastor: Friends, hear the Good News! We are dealt with mercifully.

People: The grace of our Lord Jesus is lavished upon us with the faith and love which are ours through him.

Pastor: Friends, believe the Good News!

People: In Jesus Christ, we are forgiven.

[AND]

Exhortation

Be equal to the task as you are enabled by Christ Jesus and worthy of the trust he puts in you to accomplish the service to which you are appointed.

PRAYER OF THE DAY

Provident God, your purposes are not served by waste. You rejoice when the lost is found and the disused is put to use. Help us to share your excitement at the recovery of what was out of place and to fulfill our own ministry wherever we may serve you best, through Jesus Christ our Lord. Amen

PRAYER OF THANKSGIVING

We rejoice with you, happy Parent, at the return to your house of wandering children who have squandered part of their lives in meaningless living, but now are again in the circle of your adoring family. We praise your generosity in letting bygones be bygones and not casting up our past sin in our faces. May every time we gather at your Table be a celebration of your forgiveness and every occasion of worship a festival of your grace in Jesus Christ our Lord. Amen

PRAYER OF DEDICATION

Fill our minds with your wisdom, wise God, and our hearts with sincerity, lest our offerings be a mockery and not acceptable to you. Make us willing to obey you, to teach sinners your commands so they will turn back to you; through Jesus Christ the Redeemer. Amen

PRAYER OF INTERCESSION
AND COMMEMORATION

Hear our intercessions, gracious God, for the sake of Jesus Christ, the Savior of the world.

Continue, Holy Spirit, to cleanse the church of all fault and sin, and strengthen us in resisting the temptation to depart from the truth as it is in Jesus Christ. Defend us against all slanderous attack and give us an adventurous spirit in seeking human need and meeting it from the spiritual resources that you will supply. So may your church be seen not as a naysayer but as a harbinger of good things to come.

Rebuild the church where it has dwindled and barely survives. Bless those who seek to plant the church where none now exists. Save us from the competitive spirit which may be appropriate in business but out of place in the church that Christ prayed would be one as you and he are one.

Heavenly Ruler, rule over those who are set in authority over us. Grant them wisdom, discretion, equity, and firmness, that in both counsel and action they may bring forth justice before all people high or low.

Merciful God, hear our entreaties for all who at this time are sick and sorrowful. Grant them your saving health, giving them such patience and perseverance that they may work through their afflictions to godly peace and strength.

Heavenly Father, Divine Brother, Holy Spirit, we bless you for the communion of all your saints. We remember with thanksgiving those most dear to us who for years, many or few, have served you as lights in the world and now shine beyond all earthly gloom in your heaven. Let their good example inspire our pursuit of the perfection you will grant us at last in the likeness of Jesus Christ, to whom with you be all honor and praise. Amen

Proper 20 (September 18-24)

First Lesson - The prophet laments the sad state of affairs among his people. Jeremiah 8:18–9:1

Psalm 79:1-9

Second Lesson - The apostle Paul outlines a prayer list for Timothy. 1 Timothy 2:1-7

Gospel - Jesus tells an enigmatic parable about the dangers of wealth. Luke 16:1-13

CALL TO WORSHIP

Leader: The grace of our Lord Jesus Christ be with you all.
People: And also with you.
Leader: Praise the matchless One, servants of God.
People: There is none like our sovereign God in heaven or on earth.

INVOCATION

O God of our salvation, we seek to give glory to your name through Jesus Christ and in his living Spirit. Receive our worship and hear our petitions for his sake who loved us and gave himself for us, Jesus our Lord. Amen

PRAYER OF CONFESSION

Ruler of All, all things, all persons, we admit that we are more shrewd in getting ahead in earthly things than we are in heavenly things. We may use every advantage we can get to avoid taxes, but not every opportunity to avoid temptation. We may pad our accounts and exaggerate our virtues in giving account of ourselves. Forgive dishonest accounting and slipshod morality for the sake of your Son, our Savior, Jesus Christ. Amen

Declaration of Pardon

Pastor: Friends, hear the Good News! It is the will of God our Savior that all should find salvation and come to know the truth.

People: In Christ we have found salvation and come to know the truth.

Pastor: Friends, believe the Good News!

People: In Jesus Christ, we are forgiven.

[AND]

Exhortation

Be trustworthy in little things, so that God will trust you with greater things, both in this life and in the life to come.

PRAYER OF THE DAY

Liberating God, free us from subjection to property, so that we may not be bound to money for the sake of power or privilege, but use what we have for your purposes: the enrichment of the human spirit, whether that be the spirit of others or our own spirit, through Jesus Christ our Lord. Amen

PRAYER OF THANKSGIVING

Glorious God, People-loving Monarch, your majesty does not prevent your looking after the lowly. You sent your princely Son to live among us as our mediator. We honor the ministry of Jesus Christ and any of his disciples who have lifted the weak out of the dust and brought dignity to those who were without respect. You bring children to the childless house and make a happy family. From the rising of the sun to its setting may your name be praised, Royal One, Uncommon One, Holy One, one God. Amen

PRAYER OF DEDICATION

Timeless God, you have entered into our times in Jesus Christ and are with us now and always in the Spirit. Receive these tokens of our worldly income. We will use our money so that when it is a thing of the past, we may be received into a priceless home; through the Divine Carpenter, Jesus of Nazareth. Amen

PRAYER OF INTERCESSION
AND COMMEMORATION

Gracious God, we pray for your church, the body of Christ in the world, still broken and suffering. Confirm the faith of your church, correcting its errors, broadening its sympathies, healing its divisions. As you are one, divine Parent and divine/human Offspring, so in the Spirit may your children be of one mind and intention.

Uphold all who teach in your name, that truly expounding the wisdom of Christ they may persuade the uncommitted to declare their faith in our Lord Jesus and learn to trust and follow him who is the Light of the world and our guide to God.

Be favorable to our land, O God, despite our enmities and strife, our greed and immorality. For the sake of the humble and prayerful in every land, stay your just judgments on all nations that resist the rule of Christ. Subdue warmongers and troublemakers, and teach us the practice of peace in our streets as in our state houses. Bring to places of authority leadership with the humility to seek your wisdom.

Bless all who are vested with power that they may have prudence and courage and patience. Grant prosperity to the whole world population that suitable employment and reasonable living standards may be enjoyed everywhere. Break the grip of both political and economic tyrants that freedom with responsibility may be more universally experienced.

Compassionate God, in Christ you have known the endurance of pain, and can sympathize with the suffering. Help them to rise above fear, and to look with hope for your healing with the support and care of doctors and nurses. Bless all who establish and maintain nursing homes and hospitals, and all who organize and serve in home nursing services. Save from greed those who organize health insurance plans that the best of care may be available for rich and poor alike.

Be with our friends and family who are sick, and when life and health are no longer possible, grant a peaceful death.

We are travelers through time, Eternal One, who miss those who once walked beside us. We have here no continuing city, but have confidence that you are leading us to that City which has foundations whose Builder and Maker you are. We remember with thanksgiving those you have already graciously received into heavenly citizenship and pray for patient endurance that we may also enter into unbroken communion with them, through him who died and rose again, who lives and rules with you at your right hand, and together with the eternal Spirit are one God worthy of all our worship. Amen

Proper 21 (September 25 - October 1)

First Lesson - A real estate deal is consummated as a sign of hope for the future in a time when Jerusalem was under siege. Jeremiah 32:1-3a, 6-15

Psalm 91:1-6, 14-16

Second Lesson - Paul commends the genuinely good life with contentment. 1 Timothy 6:6-19

Gospel - Jesus tells another provocative parable about the eternal hazard of greed. Luke 16:19-31

CALL TO WORSHIP

Leader: The grace of our Lord Jesus Christ be with you all.
People: And also with you.
Leader: As long as you live, praise the Royal One.
People: We sing praise to our God all our lives long.

INVOCATION

All the glory of earthly monarchs pales in contrast to your majesty in both power and compassion, immortal Sovereign. Your love in the princely Christ encourages our audience, and your Spirit's inspiration enables our worship. Receive us in the name of Jesus Christ. Amen

PRAYER OF CONFESSION

All-Seeing God, too often we close our eyes to what is going wrong in the world. We cannot see with the eyes of the very poor that we live in relative luxury, even though there are others with many times what we have. We may live to eat and soothe our nerves with music. We spend more on cosmetics than some have to buy their daily bread. We escape from honest attempts at doing something to right the wrong with sentimental drama and contrived excitements. Forgive inaction so unlike the compassion and involvement of your Son, our Savior, Jesus Christ. Amen

Declaration of Pardon

Pastor: Friends, hear the Good News! Happy is the person whose hopes are in God.

People: God loves and restores us, straightening us out.

Pastor: Friends, believe the Good News!

People: In Jesus Christ, we are forgiven.

[AND]

Exhortation

Run the race of faith. Pursue justice, prayerfulness, fidelity, love, courage, and gentleness. Take hold of eternal life.

PRAYER OF THE DAY

Speaker of all languages, help us to heed the law of Moses that we may live morally, the call of the prophets that we may seek justice for all, the Good News of the risen Christ that

175

eternal life may be the treasure that all receive through trust in your Word. Amen

PRAYER OF THANKSGIVING

Sovereign of sovereigns, you alone possess immortality. We are dazzled by your glory. The life you give to all living things is marvelous. To live in your presence is a great honor. To have inherited the faith of Jesus and the apostles is a priceless heritage. We would express our thankfulness by making a faithful confession in the presence of many witnesses and living faultlessly until our Lord Jesus Christ appear. Amen

PRAYER OF DEDICATION

Nowhere, invisible God, do we meet you more intimately than at the table of our Lord Jesus. Graciously receive our humble gifts. Transform our offerings into acts of love to one another and to the whole world; in the Spirit of Jesus Christ. Amen

PRAYER OF INTERCESSION AND COMMEMORATION

Eternal God, you have made us priests serving with our high priest Jesus Christ, so we intercede in his name for all humanity.

Hear our prayers for your whole church, in congregations, denominations, and councils of churches, national and international. Bless all who have been called to be leaders in your church on earth that they may serve you humbly, not lording it over your people. Save us from pride in what we have done when there is so much more that we could do. As we are strengthened by the aid of the Spirit when we are working your will, so may we be repentant when chastened by the Spirit for inaction or disobedience.

Speak to your people through whom you will speak, not only through the ordained leadership but through any to whom you have given insight so that speaking or writing or acting they may call the church to do what is pleasing to you in the service of our neighbors.

Ruler above all, hear our prayers for national, regional, and local officials that they may serve us honestly with respect for your law.

Hear us, gracious God, for all the sick and ailing, for the maimed and crippled, for those of unsound mind that they may have whatever healing ministries they require. Send aid to weary parents and to those who are shut-in, and visitors to those who are confined in prisons or locked wards.

Hear our prayers for family and friends who are sick and in critical health and give us reason to rejoice in their healing or in your reception of them in the hour of death.

Eternal God, the God not of the dead, but of the living, we remember with thanksgiving those of our loved ones whom you have received into the home of the blessed. Dust they were and to dust have returned but their spirits are alive and at home with you beyond our sight. Take us at the last out of all suffering and sorrow to your joyful Presence and eternal communion with all your holy people. To you, our heavenly Father, to Jesus our loving Brother, and to our Mothering Spirit, be ascribed all loving honor for ever. Amen

Proper 22 (October 2-8)

First Lesson - This lamentation mourns Jerusalem as an abandoned widow. Lamentations 1:1-6

Lamentations 3:19-26
[OR]
Psalm 137

Second Lesson - Three generations of Christian faith are noted in this letter of Paul. 2 Timothy 1:1-14

Gospel - When slavery was still accepted, Jesus continues to define the humility of discipleship. Luke 17:5-10

CALL TO WORSHIP

Leader: The grace of our Lord Jesus Christ be with you all.
People: And also with you.
Leader: Let us sing of mercy and justice as we give sincere praise to God.
People: It is good that one should wait quietly for the salvation of the Lord.

INVOCATION

Unchanging God, your steadfast love never ceases, and your mercies never come to an end. We appreciate your mercies that are new every morning; great is your faithfulness. Receive our worship as we come to you through Jesus Christ our Savior and Lord. Amen

PRAYER OF CONFESSION

Universal Judge, we are appalled at the violence and devastation that are to be seen in our world. We find it simpler to question your patience with humanity than to take some responsibility for what we could do to calm the distressed, relieve the anger of the disturbed, or pacify the hostility of the aggressive. Forgive our lack of hope that the future could be better than the past and that our faithfulness could make some difference; through your ever-hopeful Son, Jesus Christ. Amen

Declaration of Pardon

Pastor: Friends, hear the Good News! Our eternal salvation has been brought fully into view by the appearance on earth of our Savior, Jesus Christ.

People: Jesus Christ has broken the power of death and brought immortality to light through the gospel.

Pastor: Friends, believe the Good News!

People: In Jesus Christ, we are forgiven.

[AND]

Exhortation

Stir into flame the glowing coals of the Spirit within you. The Spirit is given to inspire strength, love, and self-discipline.

PRAYER OF THE DAY

Liberating Lord, free us from self-imposed limitations that we may go on to do what we should as your faithful servants, carrying out your orders, without expecting praise and satisfied to do our duty. Amen

PRAYER OF THANKSGIVING

Fountain of faith, your living water flows down from holy heights to replenish our thirsting spirits. We are thankful for the faith of all who came before us in the people of God and for the inheritance of forms of prayer and praise that still bring meaning to our lives. We are happy in the company of others of like precious faith who lift us out of doubt and depression and despair. Fill us with such joy in believing that our faith may be drunk in by thirsting neighbors, even the water of life, Jesus Christ. Amen

PRAYER OF DEDICATION

Resourceful God, our assets are not as limited as we sometimes believe. Help us to give and to use to the full all that you have given into our hands. Achieve the purposes you have had for our earth before the time of creation now fully disclosed in the advent of Christ Jesus of Nazareth. Amen

PRAYER OF INTERCESSION AND COMMEMORATION

Founder of the church, continue to bless the church of your Son, Jesus Christ. Let all members of the church make it evident by their faithful worship and good work that your church is one family everywhere in the world. Enable all who preach and teach and share their faith to do so with the integrity and zeal the Spirit inspires.

Refresh our commitment to you with the bread you sent from heaven and the cup of the new covenant so that we may not become weary in well doing.

God of martyrs and saints, save your people who live in lands where your church is persecuted by governments or peoples. Defend them from the rage of their enemies, and grant them unwavering faith that in life or death they may bear faithful witness to your gracious forgiveness.

We pray for our country and ourselves. Stiffen our wills to do your will and to resist all evil compromise. Spread among us simple faith, sexual purity without prudishness, justice without inclemency, firmness without arrogance.

Bless our national leaders and their families. Keep them safe from harm and firm in their intention to do what pleases you. May they be an example of true piety to all the families of the nation. May our laws and our judges be a strong defense for the wronged, however poor and needy, and a terror to evil-doers, however great and mighty. Let virtue and truth be the pillars of the state.

We pray for the sick and suffering in our homes and hospitals and all known and dear to us. Save them from dejection and despair. Give them hope in your healing and patience to wait for your help.

Into your gentle hands we commend the spirits of the dying. We will live again through the same Spirit who raised our Lord Jesus from the dead, giving him glory at your right hand, O God. We bless you for the unbroken communion we have with those whom you have taken to yourself. They are safe in your holy keeping, and you will bring us also at the last to the joy and peace of your presence with exceeding joy. All praise be given you, fatherly, brotherly, motherly God. Amen

Proper 23 (October 9-15)

First Lesson - Jeremiah sends words of encouragement to the exiles in Babylon. Jeremiah 29:1, 4-7

Psalm 66:1-12

Second Lesson - The resurrection empowers the apostle to accept imprisonment and hardship with confidence. 2 Timothy 2:8-15

Gospel - Only one of ten lepers that Jesus healed—a Samaritan—comes back to thank Jesus for his new health. Luke 17:11-19

CALL TO WORSHIP

Leader: The grace of our Lord Jesus Christ be with you all.
People: And also with you.
Leader: Bless our God, good people. May the sound of our praise be heard by our God.
People: God has kept us among the living and has led us on our way.

INVOCATION

Receptive and responsive God, hear and answer our prayers as in your wisdom you know what is best for us. Urge us by the Spirit to full obedience and ready service through the church of your dear Son. Amen

PRAYER OF CONFESSION

Universal God, we are continually tempted to confine you to a certain place and time, to a past experience. Forgive the limitation by our faith that does not expect you in our present and in our future as in our past; through Jesus Christ who is the same yesterday, today, and forever. Amen

Declaration of Pardon

Pastor: Friends, hear the Good News! Even if we are faithless, Christ keeps faith, for he cannot deny himself.

People: We too may attain the glorious and eternal salvation which is in Jesus Christ.

Pastor: Friends, believe the Good News!

People: In Jesus Christ, we are forgiven.

[AND]

Exhortation

Try hard to show yourself worthy of God's approval, as a laborer who need not be ashamed. Be straightforward in your declaration of the truth.

PRAYER OF THE DAY

Compassionate Christ, as we have been touched by your love, help us to show you our thankfulness by also reaching out to others that you may touch them also through us. Amen

PRAYER OF THANKSGIVING

God of all places, you sent Jesus of Nazareth to show your loving presence in places of sickness, sorrow, and shame, to bring healing, comfort, and dignity. We are grateful for all experiences in which we encounter you. We praise your name, sender of rain and sun, Maker of rainbows, Light without shadow. Amen

PRAYER OF DEDICATION

Your church, connecting Spirit, is meant to be a non-profit corporation. Enable us to serve you so selflessly that the world will know that your body, the church, is also willing to be broken for the sake of the world. Amen

PRAYER OF INTERCESSION AND COMMEMORATION

Eternal God, fill the whole church of Christ with your presence, that it may be the light of the world, radiant with the grace of your Son, Jesus Christ, the Bright and Morning Star.

Holy God, source of all just power, defend, bless, and sustain those who govern us. Give wisdom to all judges and legislators that our laws may be justly written and fairly interpreted.

Teach all people to do to others as they would have others do to them, so that our enmities may end, our work be productive, and our benefits fair. Deliver us from immorality and greed, from gluttony and addictions to harmful drugs. Save us from all the sins that so easily beset us.

Gracious God, hear our entreaties for our kinfolk and neighbors who are sick or victims of accident. Grant them healing and health with a thankful spirit. Relieve the fears of those who look to you for aid. Bring relief to those who are in dire want and do not know where to turn. Give patience to the aged and those worn down by chronic illness. Send visitors to those who are lonely and in need of a friend. Lighten with hope the spirits of the dying that beyond their final suffering they may envision the joy you have prepared for all who love you.

Father of lights, with whom there is no variation or shadow due to change, who has received into unending peace so many of your faithful people, we give thanks for them and your brightness that was reflected from them in

183

their life with us. Replenish our spirits by your Spirit that our lamps also may shine in this dark world until we too are taken to the land where there is no night of evil but speechless glory. To you Light of heaven, to you Light who came into the world, to you Light in the church, to you, one God, be directed our thanksgiving and worship forever and ever. Amen

Proper 24 (October 16-22)

First Lesson - After all the gloom the prophet offers the hopeful promise of a new covenant. Jeremiah 31:27-34

Psalm 119:97-104

Second Lesson - The apostle Paul encourages Timothy to continue in his studies of the Holy Scripture and remain faithful to its teaching in the face of opposition. 2 Timothy 3:14–4:5

Gospel - Perseverance in prayer is urged by a story of a persistent widow seeking justice before an ungodly judge. Luke 18:1-8

CALL TO WORSHIP

Leader: The grace of our Lord Jesus Christ be with you all.
People: And also with you.
Leader: Hear and become familiar with the sacred writings which have power to make you wise.
People: The Bible can lead us to salvation through faith in Jesus Christ.

INVOCATION

We come to worship, O God, in response to your Word spoken in Jesus Christ and made known to us in the church of the apostles. Receive us as faithful witnesses to the faith inspired by your Spirit and desiring to be found ready at the coming of the Son of humanity, Jesus Christ. Amen

PRAYER OF CONFESSION

Vindicator of your people, you listen to us patiently. We confess the same sins repetitiously. We trust your mercy but do not persevere in our prayer for help to overcome the faults which we confess. We have not allowed enough time for the study of Scripture as discipline in right living and as effective training for good works of every kind. Forgive our stubborn resistance to the good urging of your Spirit, for the sake of our Savior, Jesus Christ. Amen

Declaration of Pardon

Pastor: Friends, hear the Good News! In the new covenant God declares: I will forgive their iniquity.

People: In the new covenant God declares: I will remember their sin no more.

Pastor: Friends, believe the Good News!

People: In Jesus Christ, we are forgiven.

[AND]

Exhortation

Keep on praying and never lose heart.

PRAYER OF THE DAY

Invigorating Spirit, strengthen us in the faith. Instruct our minds with the written Word and enlarge our vocabulary, to speak it with conviction, to give support to all who are wavering, to challenge all who doubt. Amen

PRAYER OF THANKSGIVING

Guardian of Israel, Savior of the church, we rejoice in your constant care. You have created a world that is magnificent, not without danger and excitement, but also with safeguards and places of rest. We are thankful for all who work for our physical health and safety, and for those who teach us your saving Word, preparing us for judgment day. Amen

PRAYER OF DEDICATION

Like Aaron and Hur upholding the hand of Moses and the staff of God, we uphold, Christ Jesus, the leaders you have called with us to lead us in your conflict with evil. Receive our gifts, our witness, and our service for the victory of your monarchy. Amen

PRAYER OF INTERCESSION AND COMMEMORATION

Almighty God, we humbly pray for your church throughout the world. Endue all pastors with the boldness of inspired apostles, giving them the spirit of power and of love and of a sound mind. May the leaders of the church in congregations, regional assemblies, and denominational bodies fulfill their vocation with zeal and our Lord's serving spirit. Grant to all of us who have known your forgiveness a forgiving disposition that we may speak your saving word to sinners with compassion, and bring to those who are weary consolation and encouragement. May our manner of life day by day commend Christ to those who live without faith in him.

Bless and inspire with wisdom our national leaders and their advisors, that their words and actions may honor you and respect the dignity of all people. Bless and guide the United Nations that all their meetings and activities may seek peace with justice.

You only, O God, can keep our going out and our coming in from this time on and forevermore. Keep us alert as we drive and mindful of the mistakes that can be hazardous to our safety and the safety of others. Grant a full sense of responsibility to all who operate systems of transportation on land or sea or air that they may care not only for themselves but for the well-being of passengers and other operators.

Great Physician, heal and relieve those who are sick or anxious for the health of kinfolk and friends. Grant encouragement to the depressed and sorrowful, courage to the fearful, and peace of mind to the overwrought.

You are our God forever and ever and shall be our guide even unto death. We bless you for all those whom you have received into the perfect peace of Christ. We are grateful for the happy memories of their friendship in our homes and in this sanctuary. We celebrate with joy around the table of our Lord in communion with your saints in earth and heaven. Bring us at last to the pure joys of your heavenly feast of which we have now a foretaste in bread and wine. You are worthy, our Lord and God, to receive glory and honor and power, for you created all things, and by your will they existed and were created. You are worthy, Lamb of God who was slain, to receive power and wealth and wisdom and might and honor and glory and blessing! You are worthy, divine Spirit, for we hear your welcome: "Blessed are the dead who from now on die in the Lord, . . . They will rest from their labors, for their deeds follow them." You are worthy, one God, of all our love and worship through Jesus Christ our Lord. Amen

Proper 25 (October 23-29)

First Lesson - The prophet promises that good times will compensate for hard times. Joel 2:23-32

Psalm 65

Second Lesson - The apostle Paul's second letter to Timothy draws to a close. 2 Timothy 4:6-8, 16-18

Gospel - In a parable Jesus teaches us how and how not to pray. Luke 18:9-14

CALL TO WORSHIP

Leader: The grace of our Lord Jesus Christ be with you all.

People: And also with you.

Leader: Happy are you to choose to be here, having been chosen by God to be brought near to worship in God's sanctuary.

People: We are happy to worship in God's sanctuary. We will be satisfied with the goodness of this place.

INVOCATION

Sovereign God, we come to your house to show our adoration, but only because you first loved us through Jesus Christ. We are grateful for your initiative though we sometimes wrongly take the credit for our wise choice to worship. We pray worthily only with the aid of your prayerful Holy Spirit in the name of Jesus Christ. Amen

PRAYER OF CONFESSION

Great God, mighty and awesome, you are above all pettiness and unmoved by cheap bargaining. Forgive our preference for people just like us, our suspicions of those alien to us, our double standards of caring for those of our kind and those of other customs. Excuse our neglect of justice on behalf of those who are not in a position to speak for themselves. We have forgotten your outgoing grace which found us when we were still strangers to you but you did not hesitate to send your only Son, Jesus, to find us and include us in the number of your people. We are sorry that we are not yet much like you, over-arching God, shoulder-to-shoulder God, pervasive God. Amen

Declaration of Pardon

Pastor: Friends, hear the Good News! God has mercy on sinners.

People: God acquits us of our sins, exalting the humble.

Pastor: Friends, believe the Good News!

People: In Jesus Christ, we are forgiven.

[AND]

Exhortation

Run the great race. Finish your course. Keep the faith. A garland of goodness awaits you and all who have set their hearts on Christ's appearing on that great day.

PRAYER OF THE DAY

Save us from building ourselves up at the expense of others, fair God, lest we face your final humbling. Teach us humility and honesty in self-evaluation that does not seek freedom from blame by doing nothing, but by striving to continue until we have completed the course you have set before us. Help us to recognize our constant need of your grace, even as we grow closer to you. Grant us the resurrection to final joy as you did your Son and our Savior, Jesus Christ. Amen

PRAYER OF THANKSGIVING

Initiating Spirit, Consummating Being, you never leave your people in the lurch. You have done wonderful things which your people Israel saw with their own eyes. You are the refuge of all who come to you and their relief. You give your people strength. Your church has suffered but has never been destroyed. Yor witness lasts from age to age. We rejoice in your continuing care and live in confidence that in the end the humble will be exalted and the proud be put in their place. Praise to you, the One all-knowing, the One all-feeling, the One all-healing. Amen

PRAYER OF DEDICATION

Whatever the offerings we place on your altar, Supreme Creator, accept them as the gifts of the humble. Enable and enlarge the use of all our talents as you lead us to work together, never completely alone, for you are always with us. Amen

PRAYER OF INTERCESSION AND COMMEMORATION

Heavenly Parent of all parents, receive our prayers for others through Jesus Christ whom you sent to be an elder brother to a great family of siblings.

Founder of the church, you have built us on the foundation of the apostles and prophets, Jesus Christ himself the cornerstone. Preserve and extend this structure through us like living stones, being built into a spiritual house, to be a holy priesthood, to offer spiritual sacrifices acceptable to you through Jesus Christ. Make us your prophets, speaking your word of judgment, and evangelists also proclaiming the Good News of salvation to all people who will hear.

Sovereign God, overrule the conflict of nations. Grant to the United Nations the ability to bring reconciliation between warring factions. Deliver the world from angry racism that ignores our common origins and antagonisms that ignore our common faults. Save our leaders and our country from iniquity and deceit. Build up in us a love of truth and honor, mutual respect and individual freedom. Save family life from disintegration through the inroads of promiscuity and sexual irresponsibility.

Lover of children, watch over our offspring, making us mindful that what they see in us is a primary example of what they can be. So may we in turn look to Jesus as our model and teacher, seeking to guide our children into his Way.

Be near, Great Physician, to touch the fevered brow and heal the sick and mend the body broken by accident. Multi-

190

ply the gifts of healing that we may have enough doctors and nurses and other therapists to meet the need for human health. Remember those whom we forget and all who look to us for our prayers.

Eternal God, we bless you for all your people who in life have endured as seeing you who are invisible. Grant us the patience of the saints in our time of testing that with them we may honor your commandments and in the faith of Christ win also the crown of glory which you promise to all who love you.

All glory be ascribed to you, fatherly, brotherly, motherly God, one God, forever and ever. Amen

Proper 26 (October 30 - November 5)

First Lesson - Patience is urged by the prophet saying that justice will prevail in the end. Habakkuk 1:1-4, 2:1-4

Psalm 119:137-144

Second Lesson - Paul and his two companions send greetings to the church in Thessalonica. 2 Thessalonians 1:1-4, 11-12

Gospel - Luke records a memorable conversion story in the ministry of Jesus. Luke 19:1-10

CALL TO WORSHIP

Leader: The grace of our Lord Jesus Christ be with you all.
People: And also with you.
Leader: Come in the right spirit.
People: The righteous live by their faith.

INVOCATION

Infinite and holy God, our faith brings us to you in humility to seek your hearing and to receive your blessing. Receive the

191

worship we offer in the Spirit you have shared with us in human measure by the grace of our Lord Jesus Christ. Amen

PRAYER OF CONFESSION

God compassionate and gracious, long-suffering, ever constant and true, forgive our iniquity, rebellion, and sin. We go on stubbornly in selfish ways and persist in sins that take their toll on generations to come. We risk our own health and the health of the unborn with the use of substances you did not create for our bodily use. We refuse your offered power to liberate us from enslaving habits. Forgive our unwillingness to change even for our health's sake; through Jesus Christ our Lord. Amen

Declaration of Pardon

Pastor: Friends, hear the Good News! Jesus came to pardon sinners and will bring to fulfillment every good promise.

People: Jesus will bring to fulfillment every act inspired by faith according to the grace of our God in Jesus Christ.

Pastor: Friends, believe the Good News!

People: In Jesus Christ, we are forgiven.

[AND]

Exhortation

Live in a manner worthy of your calling so that the name of Jesus may be glorified in you, and in patient and sure expectation of his coming.

PRAYER OF THE DAY

Universal Son of Man, in the church you have come far from the fold of Israel to seek and to save us. Send us to find those in our community and in our world who are lost that they may find you and be found by you, and that they may be

192

counted among the children of Abraham and Sarah, faithful believers in one God. Amen

PRAYER OF THANKSGIVING

Divine Searcher, you have come to where we are, and we rejoice in your salvation. You are good to all and your tender care rests upon all your creatures. We will talk of the glory of your peaceable kingdom and proclaim the majesty of your mighty deeds. You give with a bountiful hand and watch over all who love you. All praise and thanksgiving we give to you, God of Abraham and Sarah, God of Jesus, Mary, and Joseph, God of all the nations. Amen

PRAYER OF DEDICATION

Head of the church, we may not be rich enough to give half of what we have to charity, but we share the support of the church with other members. Grant us faith and an unselfish spirit that we may give a generous portion of what we have to others through your church and ours. Amen

PRAYER OF INTERCESSION
AND COMMEMORATION

God our Creator, you found good all that you made, and when sin spoiled your paradise you set out to regain and re-create it. At your command we pray for your whole creation especially for all your people everywhere.

So bless your church with gracious love that it may gather to you those who have neglected the great salvation you offer to all in the death and resurrection of Jesus Christ. Keep us simple in our basic faith that however complex our theology we may offer to unbelievers the plain invitation of Jesus to come to him and find abundant life. So may your church grow in numbers and in hope, receiving the humblest and

193

the youngest whom you draw to yourself and embrace with grace.

We pray for our country and its leaders that the beauties of the land and the glories of the law may not be spoiled by avarice and abuse. Minimize the need for the military in our world, but bless those still needed to guard our neighborhoods and our borders. Watch over all who go down to the sea in ships doing business on the mighty waters. Protect mariners and fisherfolk at sea, and comfort those who have suffered loss by tempest and flood.

Blessed Jesus, you make the sea calm and go to those over whom the billows roll. Call out to those swamped by temptation and in danger of going down. Save those who are perishing who cry out to you, and bring them to a quiet haven where they may be at peace and sing your praise.

We pray for the sick and ailing that you will give them strength according to their day. Sickness may plague children and youth as well as adults and the aged. Your healing presence is needed, and you heed the prayers of all who call upon you. Bless all human ministries to the sick at home or in hospitals or elsewhere. Grant rest and peace to those who are dying.

We give you thanks for all who have completed their earthly life and now live with you in heaven. We rejoice especially with those who shared part of our journey toward the City of God. May we keep faith with them and with you, completing our pilgrimage in the strength of the Holy Spirit, our Companion, to whom with you, gracious God, and to you, loving Savior, be expressed gratitude and endless thanksgiving. Amen

All Saints (November 1 or First Sunday in November)

First Lesson - Despite visions of terror the prophet also had dreams of an eternal kingdom for the people of God. Daniel 7:1-3, 15-18

Psalm 149

Second Lesson - The apostle Paul celebrates our inheritance of glory with the royal Jesus. Ephesians 1:11-23

Gospel - Luke records the woes of Jesus declared against the rich as well as blessings for the poor. Luke 6:20-31

CALL TO WORSHIP

Leader: The grace of our Lord Jesus Christ be with you all.
People: And also with you.
Leader: Exult in glory, faithful people. Let the high praises of God be in your mouth.
People: The Eternal One takes pleasure in us and adorns the humble with victory.

INVOCATION

Eternal God, we exult in the victory of Jesus Christ over death and hell in resurrection and ascension to your right hand. His victory is our hope, and with all the humble we worship you in his living Spirit. Amen

PRAYER OF CONFESSION

Sovereign God, we do not need nightmares to fill us with fear. The television news shows us some of the horrors of war and cruelty in the streets. When the promise of peace seems strongest, new conflicts between tribes and nations break out, and our world continues in turmoil awaiting the final victory of your justice and peace. Forgive our doubts that you will one day rule the world without opposition; through Jesus Christ our Lord. Amen

Declaration of Pardon

Pastor: Friends, hear the Good News! The risen Christ frees you from your sins.

People: We inherit everlasting life in the glory of all the saints.

Pastor: Friends, believe the Good News!

People: In Jesus Christ, we are forgiven.

[AND]

Exhortation

Pray that the God of our Lord Jesus Christ, the Father of glory, may give you a spirit of wisdom and revelation as you come to know him.

PRAYER OF THE DAY

Teach us, patient Jesus, to love our enemies, and do good to those who hate us. We need the grace of your Spirit to bless those who curse us and to pray for those who abuse us. Only with your help will we do to others as we would have them do to us. Amen

PRAYER OF THANKSGIVING

Ageless God, eternal Christ, undying Spirit, we give thanks for our inheritance in Jesus Christ with all the saints who have lived before our time and all other members of the church who live in our own time. What grace you have manifest to us sinners that we may share the glory of your unending dominion! For all who have brought that Good News to us we give you thanks. We rejoice in the communion of saints today and always. Amen

PRAYER OF DEDICATION

Eternal God, we offer ourselves as links in your communication chain to pass along the Good News until the end of time. Bless your church in all that it does in obedience to your plans and purposes; through Jesus Christ our Lord. Amen

PRAYER OF INTERCESSION AND COMMEMORATION

Abba, Father, your Son Jesus taught us to pray with such familiarity and also most profoundly to pray for the coming of your kingdom on earth.

Teach the rich the blessedness of generosity; give the poor the understanding that one day the proud will be bought low, and the lowly lifted up; and teach us all to share unselfishly that there may be enough of your good gifts of the earth for all.

Grant to our leaders in government a concern for people that they may seek to provide for others the benefits they take for themselves. Teach us all to do to others as we would have them do to us.

Discipline our reactions to hostility so that our response to violence may be restrained and that both our private life and our street life may be more orderly and peaceful.

Bless every program that seeks to provide for the hungry both in emergency situations and where famine is endemic. May we share both surpluses of food and skills to help the hungry raise more food for themselves.

Be with your church everywhere but especially we remember Christian minorities that are persecuted for their faith by people and governments around the world. Grant them consolations in their suffering and grace sufficient for their needs.

We rejoice in your promise that the holy ones of the Most High shall receive the kingdom and possess the kingdom forever and ever. We celebrate the communion of your people

197

in heaven and earth and hope for the day when your will may be done on earth as it is in heaven. Bring us all into one holy company, no longer separated from each other by any distance, or dimension, or disagreement that we may gather to worship you, Father, Brother, Mother, in one holy family for ever. Amen

Proper 27 (November 6-12)

First Lesson - The prophet promised that the glories of the rebuilt temple will outshine the glories of the temple now in ruins. Haggai 1:15b–2:9

Psalm 98
[OR]
Psalm 145:1-5, 17-21

Second Lesson - The very antithesis of the Christ will come, warns the apostle Paul, before our Lord Jesus Christ returns. 2 Thessalonians 2:1-5, 13-17

Gospel - Jesus answers the Sadducees' question about the resurrection with a strong counter proposal. Luke 20:27-38

CALL TO WORSHIP

Leader: The grace of our Lord Jesus Christ be with you all.
People: And also with you.
Leader: God is near to all who pray truthfully and fulfills the desire of all who pray devoutly.
People: God hears our cry and saves us.

INVOCATION

Be near to us who pray, O God, by the Spirit enabling us to be truthful and reverent. Shape our desires that we may seek your will and the salvation which includes others with us; through Jesus Christ, the Lord of the church. Amen

PRAYER OF CONFESSION

God of the living, we confess that our faith is often unimaginative. We are limited by what we know and experience in this life. We find it difficult to believe that there can be another life without the limitations of this life. We hesitate to lay up for ourselves treasures in heaven, and invest too much in what passes away at the time of our death. Forgive our shortsightedness in not envisioning the glories you have prepared for your children beyond death; for the sake of your Son Jesus, who is alive from the dead. Amen

Declaration of Pardon

Pastor: Friends, hear the Good News! The Lord's love endures forever.

People: The Lord chastens us but does not surrender us to death. God is our deliverer.

Pastor: Friends, believe the Good News!

People: In Jesus Christ, we are forgiven.

[AND]

Exhortation

May the Lord direct your hearts toward God's love and the steadfastness of Christ!

PRAYER OF THE DAY

God of the burning bush, Lord of the empty tomb, Spirit of life; in living prevent us from being consumed by our passions; in dying save us from despair; and after our death raise us to everlasting life in company with all your people. Amen

PRAYER OF THANKSGIVING

God of justice, compassion, and love, we are grateful for all judges, legislators, and executives who are devoted to justice in action and not merely in words. We give thanks for all who have shown compassion on widows and widowers and or-

199

phans and have provided for them when they were in want. We remember happily the citizens who have welcomed newcomers, strangers, and aliens and helped them find their place in a new land. We celebrate in anticipation the pleasant place you have prepared for all who love your appearing. Glory be to you, O God. Amen

PRAYER OF DEDICATION

God of the living, not only in one great hour of sharing, but in all the days of our lives, use us and our total resources to help feed the hungry, to heal the sick, to bring good news to the despondent, through Jesus Christ, our risen Lord. Amen

PRAYER OF INTERCESSION AND COMMEMORATION

Eternal God, by the apostle Paul you have urged that supplications, prayers, intercessions, and thanksgivings be made for everyone, all who are in high positions, so that we may lead a quiet and peaceable life in all godliness and dignity. This is right and is acceptable in your sight, God our Savior, for you desire everyone to be saved and to come to the knowledge of the truth. You are one God, and there is one mediator between you and all humanity, Christ Jesus, himself human, who gave himself a ransom for all.

Lord of the church, keep all believers by the Spirit in harmonious communion, agreeing on the basic truth, and seeking to love as you love all humanity. May the preaching and living of the gospel bring to faith in Christ all who remain in disobedience and disbelief. Save us from dogmatism, pride, and divisiveness that we may be humble disciples sharing our riches in Christ with those who have not yet laid claim to that treasure.

We pray for the world and all its people, but especially for our nation and its citizenry. Grant true dignity to our leaders

200

that they may govern us with grace and wisdom enacting good laws for the benefit of all and not the few but powerful.

You have made a world where we may join together to do things that cannot be done alone. In business and industry bring cooperation between those who labor and those who manage. Do not let greed bring injustice that spawns hatred and violence. May income be fair for all and work worth doing. Save us from exploitation both in the workplace and in the marketplace, that our society may live peaceably.

Remember, O Lord, those who are sick in body, mind, or spirit, and in particular those we name in the silence of our hearts. Relieve suffering, heal their hurting, and give them joy instead of sadness.

Receive in tranquility the departing spirits of those who leave this life for the life with you. We rejoice that nothing can break the sacred ties that bind us as one family in heaven and on earth. Sustain us with the Easter hope of everlasting life until our separation is ended and we are re-united with those from whom we have been parted by death.

To you, O God, we present our supplications and intercessions through Jesus Christ your Son, to whom with you and the Holy Spirit be the glory and praise now and evermore. Amen

Proper 28 (November 13-19)

First Lesson - The prophet foresees the new heavens and the new earth as a place of joy and peace. Isaiah 65:17-25

Isaiah 12

Second Lesson - The apostle Paul gives the Thessalonians a strong recommendation that they be steadfast in their daily work as they anticipate the unknown day of the return of Jesus. 2 Thessalonians 3:6-13

Gospel - Jesus encourages endurance under persecution that will surely come. Luke 21:5-19

CALL TO WORSHIP

Leader: The grace of our Lord Jesus Christ be with you all.

People: And also with you.

Leader: Sing praises to the Eternal One, who has done gloriously.

People: We will let this be known in all the earth, for great in our midst is the Holy One of Israel and the church.

INVOCATION

Holy God, you have come in our midst through Jesus Christ and to the heart of the church by the Holy Spirit. We have gathered again to praise your glorious grace and truth manifest in Jesus Christ, in whose name we pray. Amen

PRAYER OF CONFESSION

Your work, Eternal One, is beyond our grasp. We confess that we are often reluctant to work. We lose the satisfaction of rest after a job well done. We are too willing to let others do what we have time and opportunity to do. Forgive us if we neglect our own work to mind others' business, if we interfere in the affairs of others instead of pulling our own weight. We forget that the night is coming when no one can work. Forgive us for the sake of your Son, the Nazarene carpenter, who finished what you sent him to do. Amen

Declaration of Pardon

Pastor: Friends, hear the Good News! Surely God is your salvation.

People: We will trust and not be afraid.

Pastor: Friends, believe the Good News!

People: In Jesus Christ, we are forgiven.

[AND]

202

Exhortation

Stand firm in the faith. Do not be misled by false prophets of doom. Do not panic when the news is bad. By standing firm you will win true life for yourselves.

PRAYER OF THE DAY

Gentle Jesus, certain and strong, save us from uncertainty and overwhelming fears. Give us the wisdom of truth which no one can refute, and a strong voice to speak up against falsehood and slander. Though others betray us, keep us faithful to you. Amen

PRAYER OF THANKSGIVING

God of crisis, God of everyday, God of eternity, we prefer vistas of beauty around us, but we are grateful for warning signs that make us more attentive to the hazards of a careless road of life. We give thanks for all who have set an example for us of certainty and assurance in the midst of trouble, conflict, and disaster. In emulating them we will come to the end of our journey rejoicing. Amen

PRAYER OF DEDICATION

Make us productive, Great Householder, accomplishing the work you have set before us to do. We would be about your business and provide our share of the resources needed for your church to work effectively and without pause, sustained by the eternal Spirit of Jesus Christ. Amen

PRAYER OF INTERCESSION AND COMMEMORATION

Sovereign God, you have bidden us to pray not only for ourselves but for all humanity. We pray for your holy church everywhere in the world that all your people may pray without ceasing, living in your presence with the Spirit to enable them with humility to hold up the cross of Jesus Christ as the hope for all sinners. Hasten the day when the head that once was wreathed with thorns shall be crowned by the worshipful obedience of all peoples.

Bless all honorable governments and overturn tyranny wherever it may be found. Grant your favor to all who seek to govern in accordance with your law, ruling justly, with mercy.

Sustain all who give themselves to serve those in need: those who teach immigrants, social workers who care for the poor and the incompetent, church visitors who attend to shut-ins, public health nurses who care for the elderly and disabled in their homes. Bless all our clinics, nursing homes, hospitals, and health services that your work of healing may continue among us.

Merciful Parent, heal your children who look to you for new health and strength and who ask us to join them in their prayers. Be near to those for whom there is no more earthly help and receive them into life without suffering.

"Blessed are the dead who . . . die in the Lord," says the Spirit, "they will rest from their labors, for their deeds follow them." "In the eyes of the foolish they seemed to have died, and their going from us to be their destruction; but they are at peace, . . . because God tested them and found them worthy." We pray, good Lord, to be kept in their faith, that we too in our time may be worthy in Christ to live with them and to see the King in his beauty and the tree of life with its leaves for the healing of the nations. To you, paternal, fraternal, maternal God, be honor and dominion, time without end. Amen

Christ The King - Proper 29 (November 20-26)

First Lesson - The prophet declares that the God of Israel will have to gather the scattered flock of people driven away by their irresponsible human shepherds. Jeremiah 23:1-6

Luke 1:68-79

Second Lesson - All Christians share in the inheritance of the royal Jesus. Colossians 1:11-20

Gospel - A criminal's cross is a grotesque enthronement for the King of the Jews. Luke 23:33-43

CALL TO WORSHIP

Leader: The grace of our Lord Jesus Christ be with you all.

People: And also with you.

Leader: Follow Christ into the way of peace,

People: for by the tender mercy of our God, the dawn from on high has broken upon us, to give light to those who sit in darkness and in the shadow of death.

INVOCATION

God of light, we worship you because your Son has become the sunshine of our world, bringing us illumination in the darkness of doubt and hope in the shadow of death. Receive our prayers inspired by the Spirit of the risen Christ. Amen

PRAYER OF CONFESSION

God of the universe, we confess that we forget your concern for everyone and everything because we are so attentive to ourselves, our own families, our own congregation, our own denomination, our own country. Forgive such narrowness that ignores the magnitude of your reconciling work in Jesus Christ, King of Israel, Prince of the universe. Amen

Declaration of Pardon

Pastor: Friends, hear the Good News! God has chosen to reconcile the whole world

People: by making peace through the blood shed by Jesus Christ on the cross.

Pastor: Friends, believe the Good News!

People:**In Jesus Christ, we are forgiven.**

[AND]

Exhortation

Give thanks to the Parent par excellence, who has made you fit to share the heritage of God's people in the realm of life.

PRAYER OF THE DAY

Royal One, crowned with thorns, remember us when you come into your kingdom, preparing us now by your gracious Spirit to live with you in Paradise. Amen

PRAYER OF THANKSGIVING

Great David's greater Son, we praise your name that you rule us with the gentle caring of a shepherd. You have watched over us from the vantage point of our humanity, accepting mortality though your basic nature is unending life. Though we cannot understand the wonder of your being, yet we can praise you and give thanks for the promised victory of your rule over sin and death. King of the Jews, Prince of heaven, Sovereign of sovereigns, we worship you. Amen

PRAYER OF DEDICATION

Christ of God, you gave your life in making covenant with us that we should be your people and you our King. We can serve you with nothing less than our lives. Amen

PRAYER OF INTERCESSION
AND COMMEMORATION

O God, you have commanded us to pray no less for others than for ourselves; hear our humble intercessions in the name of Christ. Remember in blessing your whole church, and grant it purity of life and doctrine, in purity peace, in peace unity, and in unity strength that your salvation may be known to all and the whole world become the happy kingdom of your Son, Jesus Christ.

Remember our country, O God, and guide those who pilot the ship of state through many dangerous waters. May your law be their compass and your Word their chart. Prosper every good venture and lawful enterprise. Bless every effort to restore the health of our environment. Strengthen every movement that seeks to overcome unjust conditions of human exploitation. Break the power of organized vice and crime. Help our nation to live in reverence before you and in appreciation of the rights of everyone. Remember, O Lord, all who are depressed through sickness or fatigue or grief. Encourage and heal them. Lead us all to an ordered life that minimizes the hazards to our health and peace of mind.

Remember, O God, our family and friends, whether in this community or absent from us. Strengthen the ties that bind us through our letters and phone calls and visits.

We remember with undying love our parents, brothers, sisters, children, and friends who have gone home to you. We live in the hope of seeing them again in your presence where our joy will be full to overflowing.

Now to him who by the power at work within us is able to accomplish abundantly far more than all we can ask or imagine, to him be glory in the church and in Christ Jesus to all generations, forever and ever. Amen